RÖCKENWAGNER

RÖCKENWAGNER

Hans Röckenwagner

with Brigit Legere Binns

Ten Speed Press
Berkeley, California

To my mother, for all those twenties you slipped me when I was an apprentice earning only 60DM a month. And to my sister Susi, whose friendship means the world to me.

Ten Speed Press
Box 7123
Berkeley, California 94707

Distributed in Australia by E. J. Dwyer Pty. Ltd., in Canada by Publishers Group West, in New Zealand by Tandem Press, in South Africa by Real Books, in Singapore and Malaysia by Berkeley Books, and in the United Kingdom and Europe by Airlift Books.

Book design by: Rey International, Los Angeles, CA
Interior photography by: Patrice Meigneux, Santa Monica, CA
Line illustrations by: Alice Harth, San Francisco, CA
Artwork credits: pages 3, 4, and 27: display case by Hans Röckenwagner; pages 12,13, 90, 91, 142, and 143: mural by Richard Kriegler; pages 26–27: painting by Manfred Muller, Gallery of Contemporary Photography; pages 26, 27, 58, 59, 96, 97, 128, and 129: stammtisch table by Laddie John Dill; page 37: fountain by Paul Chilkov; pages 44–45: wine rack by Hans Röckenwagner; pages 48–49: wooden asparagus by Hans Röckenwagner; pages 62–63: painting by Peter Alexander; pages 74–75: chair by Greg Fleischman; pages 122, 123, 612, and 163: ceramicware by Roseline Delisle; pages 134–135: humidor by Hans Röckenwagner; pages 164–165: statue by Robert Graham; pages 178–179: check presenter by Hans Röckenwagner; pages 184–185: painting by Bill Barminski, the Robert Berman Gallery.
Quote on page 7 copyright © 1985 by the *Los Angeles Times* reprinted with permission.

Library of Congress Cataloging-in-Publication Data
Röckenwagner, Hans.
Röckenwagner, / Hans Röckenwagner with Brigit Binns
p. cm. Includes index. ISBN 0-89815-875-3
1. Cookery, American—California style. 2. Cookery, German.
3. Röckenwagner (Restaurant) I. Binns, Brigit Legere II. Title
TX715.2.C34R63 1997
641.59794 — DC21   96 – 37455 CIP

Printed in Hong Kong — First printing, 1997

1 2 3 4 5 6 7 8 9 10 — 01 00 99 98 97

Many thanks to:

Maureen and Eric Lasher, my agents who have become my family; Brigit Binns, whose knowledge, judgement, and tireless effort made this book happen; Patrice Meigneux and Roy Jensen, for their beautiful photography; Editor Lorena Jones, Publisher and Vice President Kirsty Melville, Ten Speed Owner Phil Wood, and Vice President-at-Large Jo Ann Deck, for believing in me; Joan Nielsen for her help testing the desserts; Jovan Trboyevic for bringing me to the U.S. in the first place; my former partner, Mary Fama, a great mother and the first person to coax me into sampling ethnic flavors from around the world; to Mary's entire family, especially Gene and Sally Fama, who not only put up the money for our first restaurant, but also created our bestselling Sally Fama Garden Salad; my dad, for pushing me out of the house; my kids (who are the greatest), Gina, Roxy, and Hansi, who keep me up to date on all the snack foods; the talented local artists who lent their work for the photographs in this book; all my family in Germany; the many loyal customers, who have supported me for the last $11^{1}/_{2}$ years; the core *stammtisch* group—Dona, Doug, Bob, Narda, Patty, Claudia, Teri, Christine, Steve, Bill, and Arnold; some of the very best friends a person could ever have—Marcia Hrichison, Teine Kinney, Maya Garbassi, and Gordon and Julie Lee; my entire staff, past and present, particularly Trey, Eric, Marc, Pandee, Dona, Ralfi, Hans Dieter, Dietmar, and most especially, Ellie Leisinger, Carlos Martinez, and Mario Lopez, who turned Rocken..."what?" into Röckenwagner; and Jill Pettijohn, for her help on this book.

And last, but not least, thanks to California for the fruits of the San Joaquin Valley; the wines of Napa, Sonoma, and Santa Ynez; and the cultural diversity that continues to make this a land of excitement and opportunity.

First [the waiter] set a plate before me, beautifully decorated with leaves of spinach and slices of mango. Little pink peppercorns danced across the green leaves as he ladled lobster sauce across the design. Then Hans Röckenwagner came dashing out of the kitchen cradling the crab soufflé that he spooned lovingly onto the plate. On its own, the soufflé was delightful, but tasted with the sweet unctuous richness of the mango and the spicy, almost piney flavor of the pink peppercorns the flavor mellowed, became more forceful.

...Clearly this restaurant was unique, not the copycat cuisine we so often find these days, but really original food. The chefs here have a style all their own, and each course [is] carefully thought out, beautifully arranged, presented with pride.

Ruth Reichl, restaurant critic for the *Los Angeles Times*

When this review was published, I had no idea how warmly Los Angelenos would receive me, Hans Röckenwagner from Schliengen, Germany. One week before the review ran, the restaurant was virtually empty. One week afterward, the tables were filled. We haven't looked back since then.

Even though my career has taken a less-than-typical path for a classically trained European chef, it began in the usual fashion. I spent my first three years of training in a traditional German program, working so hard that I almost forgot cooking is fun. From there I went on to spend one and a half years at the Beau Rivage Hotel and La Grappe d'Or in Lausanne, Switzerland, where I had the chance to cook alongside some of Europe's top chefs. In 1984, only three years out of the training program, I found myself at Le Perroquet, one of Chicago's top five restaurants. As the chef there, I finally had the opportunity to set a menu, and I started by lightening and freshening things up. When I arrived all the sauces were butter-based, and each main course featured the same vegetable accompaniment. I started to make vegetable coulis from tomatoes and mushrooms or whatever was fresh in the market. By the time I left, every dish had a different, specially tailored accompaniment, a detail that has come to characterize my cooking.

It was while I was at Le Perroquet that I met my former partner, chef Mary Fama. She was the first to encourage me to try the foods of other cultures with a view to the value they could have for my cooking. Of course I had always known about Chinese and Japanese food, but I had never considered the influence they had on haute cuisine. So I spent some time focusing on Asian spices and flavorings such as ginger, curries, sesame oils, chiles, and soy sauce, and the exacting presentations of sushi, which had always spoken to my interest in

the visual aspect of food. I found that my ideas were growing beyond the confines of a traditional French restaurant—it was time I became not only a chef but an owner, too.

In the mid-1980s, California was on the cutting edge of the culinary revolution in American regional cuisine, and I knew it was where I wanted to be. Many of the chefs who opened new restaurants in Los Angeles at that time had worked with established stars before they attempted to develop their ideas and visions independently. I moved to the city with no patron, no legacy of working with a star, which meant I had no preestablished clientele, but also that I didn't have to follow anyone else's lead. Perhaps naively, I set out to create a reputation based on nothing more than my ability and desire to challenge and expand standard presentations and flavor combinations.

When the first Röckenwagner opened, the menu was predominately French, even though my effort to explore other cuisines had intensified after I arrived in Los Angeles. Walking around Chinatown, Little Tokyo, and Olvera Street, sampling the city's ethnic melting pot, I began to reinterpret dishes, playing with flavors until I had something that fit my style. I've never been afraid of change, as long as it was justified.

When I am asked to define my food, I say it is a mixture of old European and Pacific

Rim cuisines, although it's changing all the time. That's why at Röckenwagner you can order a "pretzel" burger with Swiss cheese, onions, and french fries or a rock shrimp samosa with lemon chutney and cucumber raita for lunch. The most common adjectives I hear others use to describe my food are "earthy" and "sophisticated," and that pleases me. I love the earthiness of an apple pancake with crème fraîche, an onion tart or sautéed trout on toasted brioche with green apple, celery root, and horseradish salad. At the same time, I want the sophistication of duck foie gras ravioli with spicy plum wine sauce or white asparagus with tuna carpaccio and ginger remoulade. And when I make something basic, I give it a new twist while preserving its defining characteristics. For example, when I make potato chips, I sandwich tiny specks of fresh thyme between paper-thin slices of potato. I've never been inclined to settle down to a single theme or culinary tradition because that would simply be too limiting.

In observance of my German heritage, I modeled Röckenwagner's interior on a village square in the Black Forest. Because I love to design and build furniture, I created all the lighting fixtures and chairs. Every Christmas I make a tree-shaped candelabra to light the front window. When I had more spare time, I carved an eleven-foot, bright green wooden asparagus, which is usually propped up in a corner somewhere. My restaurant is not just a place to eat dinner; it's a place for breakfast with the family, lunch with friends, Tuesday night jazz, and birthday and anniversary celebrations. Just inside the front window we have a large *stammtisch* table, which was specially built for the restaurant by the world-renowned local artist Laddie John Dill. It's difficult to translate the word stammtisch— it means an old traditional community table. A stammtisch is not just for eating, it's also a place for celebration, work, discussion, and drinking. My stammtisch seats about sixteen, but some nights it seems there are four times as many people gathered around it. The food we serve there tends to be informal, mostly things that go well with beer like croquettes, polenta fries, exotic sausages, and other snacks and hors d'oeuvres. That's where I like to serve the food of my heritage (either authentic or slightly reworked), because the table itself is a great German tradition.

Back in the kitchen, we cure our own salmon, smoke our poultry, and make flavored oils and essences while pots of chutney bubble away on the stoves. But ours is not a menu you'd ever find in a German cafe. Breakfasts and lunches may be earthy and comforting, but they have an air of refinement; a tangy goat cheese encrusted with walnuts resting on a bed of pink grapefruit salad might be followed by a towering lamb sandwich with grilled onions and roasted peppers on wedges of five-grain focaccia bread spread with chipotle mayonnaise. At dinner the selections are more sophisticated and presentation takes a quantum leap. One of my signature dishes is the crab soufflé that the *L.A. Times* restaurant critic was so taken with. Another favorite is a free-range chicken stuffed with ham and goat cheese served with parsnip pancakes and applesauce.

Because my father was a butcher, I developed an appreciation for high-quality meat, fish, poultry, and game at an early age. I still love to cook a beautiful fillet of beef wrapped in rice paper with a truffled crust, or a rosy center of lamb loin in a tian of spinach, mushrooms, and tomatoes, but occasionally I prefer to make meat secondary to vegetables and grains. I find that many of my guests' preferences are changing as well. I don't know many strict vegetarians, but I do have a lot of friends and customers who are discovering the versatility of vegetables, grains and starches, potatoes and pasta. For me these components are just as important, if not more so, in composing a spectacular meal. Crisp noodle cakes and black bean sauce, a citrus couscous, golden pretzel knodel, a ragout of artichokes, pearl onions, and asparagus... these dishes deserve to be the stars of their own menus!

It's important that a chef not forget who he is cooking for—people who love good food are the lifeblood of any restaurant. It's not media, celebrity affiliations, or endorsements that make a reputation, but the fact that someone will come back every week for years and tell all his or her friends about you. I'll never forget the energy and anticipation I felt the night before our official opening. The restaurant was filled with friends and supporters, the dishes were new, and I was proud. The sound of happy and satisfied guests was music that still reverberates in my ears.

Running Röckenwagner is a hands-on job for me—you'll almost always find me in the kitchen, not in a studio somewhere or opening more restaurants. I want to be "on the line," making sure the crab soufflé has the perfect slightly jiggly consistency when it is served. I want to be able to fiddle with a dish if I think there is room for improvement, then watch the customers smile as they take their first bite. My personality and German sensibilities dictate how I run the restaurant and cook—it's not a classical French kitchen with a hierarchy set in stone, but there is no room for anything but strict attention to detail and the best ingredients.

I believe that once you know the basics everything else comes easily, and I train my staff to have the same philosophy. It's true that a professional has an advantage over an amateur, but anyone who enjoys great food can create a wonderful dinner with the necessary tools.

What are the tools, besides a good heavy pan and a few wooden spoons? They include a trained palate, a love of food, internal and external sources of inspiration, the excitement that comes from eating in a good restaurant, and, of course, a set of impeccable recipes.

In this book I am giving you the recipes, but I'm also leaving some of the creativity to you. I want to show you the visual highlights of my cooking and tell you how to reproduce these dishes at home if you have the time and motivation. I also want to share the simpler dishes, like sandwiches that go together in just a few minutes and always taste great. If you prepare some of the pantry ingredients, such as the chutneys, oils, and marinated vegetables, and keep them on hand, you will have even more options when experimenting with the recipes.

Don't feel as though you have to cook a dish exactly as directed or make all the components I do. Mix and match the starches, salads, and sauces to suit your tastes and menu needs—that's why I have divided each dish into subrecipes. There are hundreds of possibilities, and you're the boss. All you have to do is cook the way you like to eat.

We have always had to eat to survive, but when survival became a little bit easier, we found we wanted to eat for pleasure. The pleasure I get from cooking, from combining foods and exploring new possibilities, and from savoring the tried and true, is more rewarding than any other pursuit I can imagine. To cook for someone is a gift; it's the ultimate proof of your desire to give someone a memory that lingers long after the table is cleared.

The wonderful array of ingredients available now, the desire to eat more healthfully, the influences of my European and German backgrounds, and the convergence of different cultures in Southern California inspire and send me climbing toward new heights every day. This book retraces the path I have taken up to this point and shows where I am headed. I hope it enables you to sample the excitement and satisfaction I have enjoyed along the way, and to share it with others.

MORNING FAVORITES

German Apple Pancake with Crème Fraîche

Yield: 4 servings

We've had these apple pancakes at Röckenwagner since we opened and I think they are fantastic, especially for lunch. One of the things my mom cooked well was apple pancakes. She used to slice the apples into disks so that they had a little hole in the center where the core was. Then she just dipped them in the batter and pan-fried them. That's a little different than the way I like to do it now (mine is more like an upside-down apple pancake), but I have wonderful memories of her apple pancakes.

Pancake Batter

7 large eggs
1 tablespoon pure vanilla extract
³/₄ cup granulated sugar
¹/₂ cup all-purpose flour
1¹/₂ teaspoons baking powder

Apples

2 tablespoons unsalted butter
3 Golden Delicious apples, peeled if desired, cored and cut into ¹/₂-inch wedges
1¹/₂ teaspoons ground cinnamon
1¹/₂ tablespoons granulated sugar
1 tablespoon confectioners sugar
¹/₄ cup crème fraîche
1 cup strawberries, for garnish

Batter. In a blender or food processor, combine the eggs, vanilla, and sugar and blend for about 15 seconds, or until combined. Add the flour and baking powder and mix for 60 seconds more, or until very smooth.

Apples. Preheat the broiler to medium-high heat. Heat a 12-inch nonstick skillet over medium heat and add the butter. Add the apples and sauté for 4 to 5 minutes, or until softened. Add the cinnamon and sugar, sprinkling them evenly over the apples, and stir for 2 minutes, or until the apples are glazed and slightly translucent at the edges.

Assembly. Distribute the apples evenly in the skillet and pour the batter over them. (You may also make four individual pancakes, using a smaller pan. Just use one-fourth of the apples and one-fourth of the batter for each.) Cook until the bottom seems quite firm, about 8 minutes. Transfer the pan to the broiler and, while watching carefully, cook until the pancake is firm throughout and golden on top. Cut the pancake into 4 wedges and transfer them, apple side up, to serving plates. Sprinkle with the confectioners sugar, place a dollop of the crème fraîche on top, and garnish with the strawberries.

Homemade Granola

Yield: 8 cups

Consider this recipe a guideline and experiment until you find a mix you like best. This is a great light breakfast for the morning after a heavy dinner.

4 cups rolled oats
1/2 cup shelled sunflower seeds
1/2 cup walnut pieces
1/2 cup sesame seeds
1/2 cup shredded unsweetened coconut
1/2 cup pumpkin seeds
1/4 cup vegetable oil
1/3 cup honey
1/2 cup currants, optional
Fresh fruit to taste
Milk

Preheat broiler to high heat. Combine the oats, sunflower seeds, walnut pieces, sesame seeds, coconut, and pumpkin seeds and spread them in an even layer on a large baking sheet. Toast for 2 to 3 minutes, while watching carefully and shaking the pan occasionally so that the ingredients do not burn. The ingredients should be just golden and crisp. Cool, then transfer to a large container with an airtight cover.

In a small saucepan, combine the oil and honey and warm over low heat. Add half of the oil-honey mixture to the dry ingredients and toss thoroughly, then add just enough of the remaining oil-honey mixture to make the granola clump slightly. The granola should not be soupy. Add the currants and toss well to distribute evenly. Spread out the granola on baking sheets and let dry, uncovered, overnight at room temperature. The next morning (the granola may not be dry, which is all right), serve the granola in large, shallow bowls with the fruit and milk. The granola will keep in the airtight container for 1 week.

Hans's Favorite Muesli

Yield: 1½ quarts

This is my very favorite breakfast (or at least my favorite breakfast appetizer). When I worked in Switzerland years ago every restaurant, cafe, and canteen served muesli—kids there grow up eating pounds of it every month. Once you discover how easy this is to make you will probably eat pounds of it every month, too! It is best to make this a few days ahead so it can soak in the milk and apple purée. I sometimes add a few more nuts than the recipe calls for because I love them.

2 cups rolled oats
1/2 cup shelled sunflower seeds
2 cups milk, at room temperature
2 cups grated Granny Smith apple sprinkled with the juice of 1/2 lemon (about 4 medium apples)
Scant 1/4 cup honey
1/4 cup coarsely chopped hazelnuts
Tiny pinch of salt
1/4 cup raisins
Fresh berries, for garnish
Whipped cream, for garnish

Combine all the ingredients in a very large bowl and toss until evenly moistened. Cover and refrigerate overnight, then serve with the berries and whipped cream.

Almond-Crusted French Toast with Warm Fruit Compote

Yield: 4 servings

You can substitute other nuts, such as pecans, for the almonds in this dish as long as they are also chopped into rice-sized pieces. Almonds work particularly well because they can be purchased in slivered form and adhere nicely to the toast. Be sure that the bread is well drenched before it's cooked—there's nothing worse than dry French toast. Serve the compote warm or at room temperature. It tends to lose its nice fruity flavor when it's chilled.

Fruit Compote

2 cups mixed fruit (such as a combination of strawberries, raspberries, pears, plums, figs, apples, blueberries, and rhubarb), cut into approximately 1 1/2-inch slices or chunks

1/4 cup wine, champagne, or water

1 to 2 tablespoons sugar, or to taste, depending on the sweetness of the fruit

Juice of 1/2 lemon

French Toast

5 large eggs

1 1/4 cups milk

2 1/2 tablespoons maple syrup

2 teaspoons rum, cognac, or Grand Marnier, optional

6 (3/4-inch-thick) slices brioche bread or other rich egg bread (such as challah)

2 1/4 cups slivered almonds

1/4 cup unsalted butter or as needed

1/2 cup heavy cream, whipped to soft peaks, for garnish

Compote. In a medium nonreactive saucepan, combine the fruits, wine, sugar, and lemon juice. Over very low heat, simmer the mixture, stirring occasionally, for about 15 minutes, or until softened and soupy. If any foam rises to the top, remove it with a spoon. Cover and set aside at the back of the stove while you make the French toast.

French Toast. In a large, shallow bowl, beat together the eggs, milk, maple syrup, and rum with a fork. Dredge both sides of the bread slices thoroughly in the egg mixture. Spread out the almonds evenly on a tray and lay each piece of bread on the almonds, pressing down gently so that the nuts adhere to the slices. Turn the bread over and coat the other sides.

Heat a large, nonstick pan over medium-low heat and add a few slivers of butter. Cook each slice of bread for 1 1/2 to 2 minutes on each side, or until light brown. Add more slivers of butter around the edges of the pan when you turn the toast, and as needed when the butter is absorbed, so the nuts do not burn. Cut each slice in half and place 3 halves perpendicular to one another on each of 4 warm serving plates. Spoon some of the warm compote over the top and garnish with a dollop of the whipped cream.

How I Use Acidity

I believe acidity plays an important role in fine cuisine. If I don't start a dish with a dash of acidity, I add it at the end. To me, acidity is imperative in finishing the flavors in a dish; it allows the taste buds to experience the fullness of all the elements. Much of the food we love to eat is intrinsically rich. A jolt of acidity cuts the richness and offers a welcome cleansing of the palate. Throughout the Mediterranean you'll find crisp roast chicken, dripping with olive oil and butter, served with a mound of lemon wedges. Without a squeeze of lemon, this simple dish would be overly rich, even cloying.

As a food lover, you may often taste sauces that have a wonderful flavor, but are somehow flat and would not be lifted with the correct seasoning of salt and pepper. Vinegar and other acidic ingredients, such as a citrus juice, are the answer because they add depth to dishes that are refined and complex.

If you don't want to commit to changing the character of an entire batch of sauce, spoon a little into a separate container, add a drop of vinegar or citrus juice, and taste. Then, adjust the amount in the whole batch of sauce accordingly. How much? When using balsamic vinegar, which I probably use more than any other vinegar, I add about ¹/₂ teaspoon to a port wine sauce for 6 people, for instance. In a beurre blanc for 6, I add about ¹/₂ tablespoon of lemon juice. Sherry vinegar is very sharp (unless you can get your hands on a good aged variety), so I use only a tiny dash. Japanese vinegar, which I like to use on vegetables, is mild enough that I use a few generous dashes just as the vegetables finish cooking. The benefit of fine vinegars like the German wine vinegars I often use (see page 73) is that, since the acidity is so low, I can get away with adding a little more. This way I get more of the flavor of the individual vinegar without sending the dish off the acidity scale. But, I don't often use the German vinegars in sauces. They are so pure and rich that I consider them more a condiment than an ingredient.

You can drizzle a little over ice cream or use my favorite method: fill a decorative fine-misting spray bottle with vinegar and spray the dish at the table just before serving. When the vinegar settles on the hot food, it releases a powerful burst of aroma that envelops the diner in a sensual cloud.

Quite a few of my sauces feature reduced vinegar, usually balsamic. This technique concentrates the flavor of the vinegar and removes much of the acidity (it boils away as the vinegar reduces, just like the alcohol in wine evaporates when simmered). After you have reduced a vinegar until it's syrupy, you have several options: stir in an equal amount of veal stock and use this as a sauce on its own, or whisk in a few tablespoons of cold butter for an enriched version. Of course you could also stir the reduced vinegar, with or without veal stock, into any sauce to add another level of flavor.

Here's a quick-reference guide, showing which vinegars I use to balance an assortment of the basic sauces that appear in my recipes:

Sauces	Vinegars and Juices
Port wine sauce	Balsamic vinegar
Spicy plum wine sauce	Balsamic vinegar
Red tomato sauces	Balsamic vinegar
Yellow tomato sauces	Rice wine vinegar
Black bean sauce	Rice wine vinegar, lime juice
Beurre blanc	Lemon juice
Cream- and other dairy-based sauces	Lemon juice
Hollandaise	Lemon, lime, and blood orange juices
Salsa	Lime juice
Creamy dessert sauces	Blood orange juice
Soft fruit sauces (such as coulis)	Blood orange juice

Eggs Benedict with Blood Orange Hollandaise

Yield: 4 servings

This is a perennial favorite. What makes these different is the addition of the beautiful Blood Orange Hollandaise. This hollandaise is more substantial and contains more citrus juice than I usually add to sauces, but I think all the butter is balanced by the big jolt of acidity. It's a fresh and slightly tart variation of a classic sauce that can be a little heavy for today's tastes.

Blood Orange Hollandaise

4 tablespoons freshly squeezed blood orange juice,
    or 2¹/₂ tablespoons orange juice and
    1¹/₂ tablespoons lemon juice

2 large egg yolks

¹/₂ cup plus 3 tablespoons unsalted butter,
    cut into 14 equal pieces and softened

¹/₂ teaspoon salt

4 ounces thinly sliced Canadian bacon

¹/₂ teaspoon distilled white vinegar

8 large eggs

4 English muffins, split and toasted until golden,
    or 4 slices grilled English Muffin Bread (page 141)

Tiny pinch of ground cayenne pepper

Segments of blood orange, pith removed,
    for garnish

Hollandaise. In the top of a nonreactive double boiler over gently simmering water, combine the blood orange juice and egg yolks. Whisk gently for 1 to 2 minutes, or until the liquid is frothy and has barely begun to thicken. Whisk in a piece of butter, and continue whisking in the butter one piece at a time, waiting until each has been absorbed before adding the next. Do not let the mixture boil. If it gets too hot, remove the bowl from the heat for 1 to 2 minutes, while whisking continuously, until the mixture has cooled slightly. Stir in the salt and set aside.

Bacon. Preheat broiler to medium-high heat or heat a large skillet until very hot. Grill or sauté the bacon until golden and crisp on both sides, then transfer to a paper towel–lined plate to drain.

Eggs. In a large sauté pan with high sides and a tight-fitting lid, bring a generous amount of water to a simmer and add the vinegar. Turn off the heat and immediately break open 4 of the eggs, holding them just above the surface of the water and letting them drop gently into the pan. Quickly cover the pan, and leave undisturbed for about 3 minutes for runny yolks, 5 minutes for set yolks. With a slotted spoon, transfer the eggs to paper towels to drain while you bring the water back to a rolling boil and repeat with the remaining 4 eggs.

Assembly. On each of 4 heated serving plates, set 2 muffin halves (or 1 slice English Muffin Bread), toasted side up. Top each with a few slices of grilled bacon and a poached egg. Ladle two generous spoonfuls of the hollandaise over each muffin and sprinkle with the cayenne. Garnish the plates with the blood orange segments and serve immediately.

Eggs Florentine with Portobello Mushrooms and Hollandaise

Yield: 4 servings

One of my favorite variations for this dish is to add 8 slices of apple wood–smoked bacon, grilled until very crisp. Drain and place 2 slices on each muffin before adding the spinach. Apple wood–smoked bacon is now available from many butchers and specialty markets.

Hollandaise

4 tablespoons freshly squeezed lemon juice
2 large egg yolks
¹⁄₂ cup unsalted butter, cut into 14 equal pieces and softened
¹⁄₂ teaspoon salt

Vegetables

1 marinated portobello mushroom (page 197)
2 tablespoons unsalted butter
1 clove garlic, finely chopped
2 shallots, finely chopped
¹⁄₂ pound baby spinach leaves, well washed

4 English muffins, split and toasted, or 4 slices English Muffin Bread (page 141), toasted
¹⁄₂ teaspoon distilled white vinegar
8 large eggs
Tiny pinch of ground cayenne pepper

Hollandaise. In a nonreactive double boiler over gently simmering water, combine the lemon juice and egg yolks. Whisk gently for 1 to 2 minutes, or until the liquid is frothy and has just begun to thicken. Whisk in a piece of butter, and continue whisking in the butter one piece at a time, waiting until each has been absorbed before adding the next. Do not let the mixture boil. If it gets too hot, remove the bowl from the heat for 1 to 2 minutes, while still whisking continuously, or until the mixture has cooled slightly. Stir in the salt and set aside.

Vegetables. Preheat a grill or broiler to very high heat, and grill the marinated portobello for 5 minutes on each side, or until slightly charred. Transfer to a cutting board and slice thinly on the diagonal. Preheat the oven to its lowest setting. Heat a large skillet over medium-high heat and add the butter. Add the garlic and shallots and sauté for 2 to 3 minutes, or until softened. Add the spinach, cover the pan and cook until wilted (about 5 minutes), removing the lid every 2 minutes to toss the spinach.

On each of 4 serving plates, set 2 muffin halves (or 1 slice English Muffin Bread), toasted side up. Place a layer of cooked spinach on each muffin, and top with a few slices of the grilled portobello. Place the plates in a warm oven.

Eggs. In a large sauté pan with high sides and a tight-fitting lid, bring a generous amount of water to a simmer and add the vinegar. Turn off the heat and immediately break open 4 of the eggs, holding them just above the surface of the water and letting them drop gently into the pan. Cover the pan, and leave undisturbed for about 3 minutes for runny yolks, 5 minutes for set yolks. With a slotted spoon, transfer the eggs to paper towels to drain. Return the water to a rolling boil and repeat with the remaining 4 eggs.

Assembly. Gently reheat the hollandaise, if necessary. Place a poached egg on top of each muffin, ladle 2 generous spoonfuls of hollandaise over the top of each, and sprinkle with the cayenne. Serve immediately.

Sweet Potato and Pecan Waffles with Cranberry Butter

Yield: about 8 waffles

What's better than a toasty waffle straight off the iron early in the morning? In this dish the sweet potato, pecan, and cranberry create an incredible flavor combination.

I recommend using a nonstick waffle iron for this recipe (almost all waffle irons are nonstick these days), otherwise the sweet potato in the mixture can make the mixture stick and burn. When cooking a waffle, it's important to be patient: if you peek to see how it is doing, you will pull away the top layer and the waffle will split in the center or collapse slightly — it must have time to sear.

Cranberry Butter
1/2 cup fresh or frozen cranberries
   (thawed, if frozen)
1/4 cup maple syrup
1 cup unsalted butter, at room temperature

Waffles
1 small red yam or sweet potato
1 tablespoon vegetable oil
1 cup all-purpose flour
1 tablespoon firmly packed brown sugar
1 teaspoon baking powder
1/4 teaspoon salt
1 1/4 cups milk
1 large egg
1 1/2 tablespoons unsalted butter, melted
1/3 cup coarsely chopped pecans

Butter. In a small saucepan, combine the cranberries and maple syrup. Over low heat, cook the mixture, stirring frequently, for 5 minutes, or until the cranberries have popped and softened. Allow the cranberries to cool, then transfer them to the bowl of an electric mixer and add the butter. Mix at low speed until well combined, but not so long that the butter becomes uniformly pink. You should still be able to see little bits of the cranberry skin in the butter. Transfer to an attractive serving bowl, cover with plastic wrap, and refrigerate until needed.

Waffles. Preheat the oven to 350°. Rub the outside of the yam with the vegetable oil, prick it with a fork, and place on a baking sheet in the oven. Bake until very tender, about 1 hour, then cool on a rack. When the yam is cool enough to handle, scoop out the flesh and discard the skin. Set aside 2/3 cup of the flesh and reserve the rest for another use. Mash the sweet potato with a fork until it is very smooth. Lower the oven temperature to warm.

In a large mixing bowl, combine the flour, brown sugar, baking powder, and salt and blend well. In a separate mixing bowl, whisk together the milk, egg, and butter. Stir the milk mixture and the sweet potato purée into the dry ingredients (don't worry if there are a few lumps; it's better not to overblend). Fold in the chopped pecans.

Heat a waffle iron until very hot, then pour in the amount of waffle batter recommended by the manufacturer. Immediately close the cover and cook until done, according to the manufacturer's instructions. Keep warm in a low oven as you cook the remaining waffles. Using the large end of a fruit baller, scoop out a ball of cranberry butter and place on the top of each waffle. Serve immediately.

Corn Fritters with Smoked Salmon

Yield: 6 servings

These crisp free-form vegetable fritters are held together by the red onion, parsley, and basil; the batter is quite thin. When you form the fritters, just compact them slightly into a rough mass—there will still be lots of stray bits of vegetable sticking out and some will fall away and separate from the main clump. Stand back and watch out for splattering oil and corn kernels during the first minute or two of frying. This is a great way to showcase sweet, fresh summer corn.

Fritters

1 small yellow zucchini

1 small green zucchini

1½ cups fresh corn kernels (about 3 ears)

½ small red onion, thinly sliced

1 tablespoon fresh basil chiffonade
   (about 4 leaves)

1 cup loosely packed parsley sprigs

½ cup all-purpose flour

½ teaspoon salt

Freshly ground black pepper

3 tablespoons sparkling soda water

Vegetable oil for deep-frying

12 ounces smoked salmon

2 tablespoons sour cream

3 tablespoons Basil Oil (page 199)

6 chives, cut into ½ inch lengths

Fritters. To trim the zucchini, cut them lengthwise and remove the outer ¼ inch of flesh. Discard the central core and cut the outer sections into ¾ x ⅛-inch julienne.

Preheat the oven to 200°. In a large bowl, combine the corn, red onion, basil, parsley, and zucchini and toss to mix. Add the flour and toss with your hands, separating all the ingredients to be sure they are all coated evenly with flour. Add the salt, pepper, and sparkling water and combine well but do not overmix. The mixture should be airy and light.

In a large, heavy saucepan or deep-fryer, heat a generous amount of vegetable oil to 375°. Gather the batter into loose, free-form fritters (about 3 inches in diameter) and fry them 2 at a time for 1½ minutes on each side, or until golden brown. With a skimmer or kitchen tongs, gently transfer the fritters to a plate lined with paper towels. Place in the warm oven to drain while you fry the remaining fritters.

Assembly. Place a fritter in the center of each of 6 warmed serving plates. Encircle each fritter with 3 to 4 slices of salmon. Place a few dots of sour cream on the salmon slices, drizzle Basil Oil around the edges of the plates, and garnish with the chives. Serve immediately.

Jill's "Happy Pancake"

Yield: 4 servings

This pancake was developed by New Zealand–born chef Jill Pettijohn while she worked at Röckenwagner, and it remains one of our most popular dishes. The name is a little misleading—it's a very refined dish with a distinct Vietnamese flavor. You can vary the stuffing as desired; it doesn't have to be shrimp. As you have to make 4 pancakes in succession, measure and assemble the ingredients before you start cooking. You can find the fish sauce and "chili" paste at Asian markets.

Dipping Sauce

2¹/₂ teaspoons seasoned rice vinegar

¹/₃ cup Vietnamese fish sauce (nuoc mam)

3 tablespoons freshly squeezed lime juice

1 small carrot, cut into ¹/₁₆-inch dice

1¹/₂ cloves garlic, finely chopped

¹/₄ cup sugar

1 teaspoon Sambal Olek chili paste

1¹/₄ cups warm water

2 teaspoons finely chopped chives

Pancakes

³/₄ cup rice flour

¹/₂ teaspoon turmeric

1¹/₃ cups water

2 green onions, white and light green parts only, thinly sliced on the diagonal

¹/₂ red onion, thinly sliced

¹/₄ pound asparagus, thinly sliced on the diagonal

¹/₄ pound shiitake mushrooms, tough stems discarded and caps thinly sliced

¹/₄ pound small rock shrimp

1¹/₃ cups bean sprouts

Vegetable oil for frying

8 (3-inch) lengths chives

¹/₂ cup deep-fried carrot threads (page 202)

Sauce. In a medium mixing bowl, combine the vinegar, fish sauce, lime juice, carrot, garlic, sugar, and Sambal Olek. Mix, then whisk in the water and sprinkle in the chives. Set aside.

Pancakes. In a large mixing bowl, combine the rice flour, turmeric, water, and green onions. Whisk with a fork to mix. The batter should be deep yellow and the consistency of light cream. Measure the pancake batter and divide into 4 equal portions (before you measure or use the batter, make sure to whisk it again as the rice flour will settle to the bottom). Divide the red onion, asparagus, mushrooms, shrimp, and bean sprouts into 4 equal portions so that they can be used quickly. Preheat the oven to warm and lightly oil a baking sheet.

Heat a large nonstick skillet over high heat and add 2 teaspoons of the vegetable oil. Sauté one-fourth of the red onion for 2 to 3 minutes, or until softened. Add one-fourth of the asparagus and the mushrooms and stir together for another 2 minutes, or until they just begin to soften. Add one-fourth of the shrimp and distribute the ingredients evenly over the base of the pan. Pour one-fourth of the batter into the pan and swirl to distribute it evenly; it should form a very thin layer. Cover the pan and after about 2 minutes, when the pancake is starting to turn crisp and golden on the bottom, add one-fourth of the bean sprouts. Cover and steam for 1 to 2 minutes more, or until the sprouts have just begun to wilt. Lift and fold the pancake as you would fold an omelette, then transfer to the prepared baking sheet and keep warm in the oven while you cook the remaining 3 pancakes.

Assembly. Transfer each pancake into a large flat bowl and pour one-fourth of the dipping sauce around each. Top with 2 chive lengths and the deep-fried carrot threads. Serve immediately.

Chicken Hash with Mushrooms, Basil, and Poached Eggs

Yield: 4 servings

Here is my version of an American classic. In this recipe I call for one poached egg per person, but I often like to add another. When you cut into the egg, the yolk flows into the hash mixture and holds it all together on your spoon.

Chicken
3 chicken legs (both drumsticks and thighs)
Salt and freshly ground black pepper

Vegetables
1 tablespoon vegetable oil
1/2 yellow onion, cut into 1/4-inch dice
1/2 yellow bell pepper, stemmed, seeded, and cut into 1/2-inch dice
1/2 red bell pepper, stemmed, seeded, and cut into 1/2-inch dice
2 1/4 cups (about 6 ounces) firm white button mushrooms, sliced 1/4 inch thick

Hash
2 large or 3 medium potatoes, peeled, cut into 1/4-inch dice, and placed a bowl of cold water (to prevent oxidation)
2 tablespoons vegetable oil
1/4 cup loosely packed basil chiffonade (about 16 leaves)
1/2 teaspoon salt
Freshly ground black pepper to taste

1/2 teaspoon distilled white vinegar
4 large eggs

Chicken. Preheat the oven to 350°. Season the chicken legs with salt and pepper and roast in a small roasting pan for 45 minutes, or until the juices from the thigh joint run clear. Cool on a rack. When cool enough to handle, discard the skin and shred the meat, making sure to remove all the bones and cartilage.

Vegetables. Heat a large skillet over medium-low heat and add the vegetable oil. Sauté the onion for 3 to 4 minutes, or until it begins to soften, then add the bell peppers and mushrooms. Cook for 4 to 5 minutes, or until all the vegetables are softened but not mushy. Transfer the vegetables to a bowl, set them aside, and wipe the skillet with a paper towel.

Hash. Drain the potatoes well and pat dry with a kitchen towel. Reheat the skillet over medium-high heat and add the vegetable oil. Sauté the potatoes, turning them over occasionally with a metal spatula, until they are tender but not mushy, about 5 minutes. Add the pepper-mushroom mixture and the shredded chicken to the potatoes and toss together gently over low heat until heated through. Add the basil, salt, and pepper. Remove the pan from the heat and set aside, covered.

Eggs. In a large sauté pan with high sides and a tight-fitting lid, bring a generous amount of water to a simmer and add the vinegar. Turn off the heat and immediately break open the eggs, holding them just above the surface of the water and letting them drop gently into the pan. Quickly cover the pan, and leave undisturbed for about 3 minutes for runny yolks, 5 minutes for set yolks. With a slotted spoon, transfer the eggs to paper towels to drain.

Assembly. Place a generous mound of hash in the bottom of 4 large, heated serving bowls. flatten the top of the hash slightly with the back of a spoon, and top each one with a poached egg. Serve immediately.

SOUPS AND SALADS

Scallion Soup with a Grilled Baby Lamb Chop

Yield: 6 servings

I like my soups to be 3-dimensional, not flat and boring, and to have distinct textures. This visually stunning, bright green soup is a perfect example. In the restaurant we serve this dish with a potato tower filled with the butternut squash purée, which is virtually impossible to do at home. We have this wonderful $400 machine that makes long paper-thin strips of potato, and I'm afraid nothing else will do the job. When I'm preparing the dish at home, I make a nice, tall mound of the squash purée and lean the lamb chop up against it. I suggest you do the same.

Lamb Chops
1/4 cup extra virgin olive oil
1 1/2 teaspoons coarsely cracked black pepper
2 cloves garlic, finely chopped
6 baby lamb chops, Frenched

Soup
3 shallots, thinly sliced
2 1/4 cups dry white wine
1 3/4 cups heavy cream
60 scallions, green parts only
1 large bunch flat-leaf parsley, stems removed
3/4 cup milk
1/2 teaspoon salt
Freshly ground white pepper to taste

Squash Purée
1 small butternut squash, halved
1 tablespoon unsalted butter, melted
3/4 cup baked potato flesh, mashed
1/4 teaspoon salt
Freshly ground white pepper to taste
Canola oil for frying
6 large shallots, thinly sliced
6 sprigs fresh chervil, for garnish

Lamb Chops. In a large, shallow bowl, combine the olive oil, pepper, and garlic. Add the chops and coat both sides well with the mixture. Cover and marinate in the refrigerator for 2 hours.

Soup. In a medium, nonreactive saucepan, combine the shallots and wine and bring to a slow simmer over medium heat. Simmer until reduced by about half. Add the cream, stir to mix evenly, and reduce again until about 2 cups of syrupy liquid remain. Cool the mixture.

Bring a large stockpot of water to a boil. Add the scallions and blanch for 1 minute. Remove with a skimmer, then shock in a bowl of ice water. Drain on a kitchen towel.

Again, bring a large stockpot of water to a boil. Add the parsley leaves and blanch for 1 minute. Remove and drain on a kitchen towel.

In a blender, combine the blanched scallions and parsley with the milk and the cooled cream mixture and mix at high speed, scraping down the sides of the container. Blend for 2 to 3 minutes, or until the mixture is very smooth and bright green. Press the mixture through a fine sieve into the top of a double boiler set over warm water (but not over the heat). Add the salt and white pepper, cover, and set aside.

Squash Purée. Preheat the oven to 350°. Lightly oil a baking sheet. Brush the cut side of the squash with the melted butter. Bake on the prepared baking sheet, cut side up, for 45 minutes to 1 hour, or until tender. While the squash is baking, bring the lamb chops to room temperature.

continued

Scallion Soup *continued*

Scoop out the flesh of the cooked squash and measure 1¼ firmly packed cups. Reserve the remaining flesh for another use. In the bowl of a food processor, combine the squash, mashed potato, salt, and white pepper, and process into a thick purée.

Assembly. Place a heavy saucepan over high heat and add 1 inch of canola oil. When the oil reaches 375°, add the shallots and deep-fry until golden. Remove and place on paper towels to drain.

Gently reheat the scallion soup. Preheat a grill or grill pan to high heat, and cook the lamb chops for about 1½ minutes on each side for medium-rare, then let rest for 2 minutes.

Place a small mound of the squash purée in the center of each of 6 large, heated bowls. Gently ladle the scallion soup around the mounds of purée. Prop a lamb chop against each mound of squash purée and top with the deep-fried shallot rings. Garnish with the chervil and serve immediately.

Beef Goulash Soup

Yield: 6 cups

My dad used to make the best goulash soup in the world, and I use the same recipe today. It makes a complete meal with a chunk of bread and a glass of wine. After my apprenticeship in Germany, I didn't cook soups for a long time. There was one station in the kitchen where you had to make nine different soups from scratch every day for three months. They were always different soups, depending on the season, availability of ingredients, and the whim of the chef de cuisine. I've recovered now, but you'll find that my soups are a little different, a little offbeat, and that's fine for Los Angeles, where the weather doesn't lend itself to hot soup. Every once in a while we'll get a chilly evening when people do ask for soup, and I serve this homey, hearty goulash, which is one of my favorites.

It's important to cut the vegetables into small, even dice because they will be visible in the bowl and make a colorful mosaic. Sometimes I use pork butt instead of beef.

1½ tablespoons vegetable oil
1½ pounds beef skirt, cut into ¾ x ¾-inch chunks
½ cup finely diced yellow onion
2 cloves garlic, finely chopped
½ cup finely diced carrots
½ cup finely diced celery
½ cup finely diced red bell pepper
¼ cup tomato paste
1 teaspoon sweet paprika
⅓ cup all-purpose flour
¾ teaspoon salt
¼ teaspoon freshly ground black pepper
Tabasco sauce to taste

1 scant teaspoon Worcestershire sauce

1 cup red wine

3¹/₂ cups water

2 cups Veal Stock (page 189) or
   Chicken Stock (page 186)

1 cup white button mushrooms, halved and
   thinly sliced

In a large, heavy saucepan or enamel casserole, heat the oil over high heat. Sear the beef on all sides until it is brown, about 5 to 10 minutes. Reduce the heat to medium, add the onion and the garlic and stir for 4 to 5 minutes, or until softened. Add the carrots, celery, and bell pepper and cook for 3 minutes, stirring frequently. Add the tomato paste, decrease the heat to very low, and cook, stirring continuously, for 2 minutes, scraping the bottom of the pan as you stir to keep the tomato paste from scorching.

Add the paprika and the flour and continue stirring and scraping the bottom of the pan for 1¹/₂ minutes. A stiff mixture will form; it is important to keep stirring so that the flour taste cooks away without the mixture burning. Add the salt, pepper, Tabasco sauce, Worcestershire, and red wine. Stir to mix well, and bring to a simmer. Let the liquid reduce by about two-thirds, then add the water, stock, and mushrooms and bring to a slow simmer. Partially cover the pan and reduce the liquid by about one-third. The meat should be very tender, almost falling apart, and the soup should be very thick. Taste and adjust seasonings if neccessary. Serve in heated, shallow bowls.

Goulash

Although goulash, a rich, dark gravy filled with chunks of braised meat, originally came from Hungary, German cooks have whole-heartedly adopted this dish and made it a staple of their national cuisine. Some like theirs extra spicy (similar to the Hungarian version, which has a lot more paprika in it), some add potatoes, some thin it with chicken stock to make a souplike style, and some use pork instead of beef. Regardless of the variation, goulash is traditionally made from less expensive, tougher cuts of meat, which add a lovely gelatinous quality to the gravy.

Goulash can be served with hunks of crusty bread or over spätzle, buttered noodles, or even mashed potatoes. It is a deceptively challenging, sophisticated dish because it isn't easy to make a good one. Serious cooks have their own carefully guarded recipes. I think I already mentioned that my dad makes the best goulash in the world. If you try his recipe, I think you'll see why this homey, old-fashioned dish has withstood the test of time.

Clear Tomato Soup with Herb Crepes

Yield: 6 servings

This dish is only worth making if you have the sweetest summer tomatoes and freshest herbs on hand. The strongly flavored, clear broth can be garnished with shrimp, stuffed pasta, or tender vegetables, and will keep in the refrigerator for up to 3 days. I sometimes add a dash of Tabasco sauce to give the broth a little extra spice and complexity.

Herb Crepes

½ cup instant-blending Wondra flour
⅓ cup milk
⅓ cup cold water
1 large egg
1 large egg white
Pinch of salt
1 tablespoon finely chopped fresh chives
2 teaspoons finely chopped fresh parsley
2 teaspoons finely chopped fresh tarragon
4 tablespoons clarified butter (page 202)

Soup

6 pounds vine-ripened plum tomatoes, quartered
7 large egg whites, lightly beaten
1 teaspoon salt
Freshly ground white pepper to taste

Herb Crepes. In a blender or mixer, combine the flour, milk, water, whole egg, egg white, and salt and blend until smooth. Pour into a measuring cup with a lip and stir in the herbs. Cover and let rest for 10 minutes.

Heat a large nonstick skillet over medium-high heat and add 2 teaspoons of the clarified butter. Pour about ¼ cup of the crepe batter into the pan and tilt it in all directions so that a thin coating forms, then quickly pour out any excess. Cook until the bottom of the crepe is lightly browned, lifting the edges to check, then flip over and cook for 15 to 20 seconds more. Remove from the pan and set aside. Repeat for the remaining 5 crepes, stacking them on top of each other as you remove them from the pan. Roll the stack of crepes into a tube and julienne them crosswise. Set aside.

Soup. In a food processor fitted with the metal blade, purée the tomatoes for 3 to 4 minutes, pulsing on and off and scraping down the sides of the bowl as necessary, until the purée is very smooth and watery. Pour the purée into a large saucepan, add the egg whites and salt and whisk together. Slowly bring the liquid to a boil over medium-high heat, whisking continuously so that the liquid doesn't stick to the bottom of the pan. When the liquid comes to a boil, decrease the heat to very low, so that it just barely simmers, and cook completely undisturbed for 5 minutes.

Line a sieve with a double thickness of slightly dampened cheesecloth. Without disturbing the egg white crust which will have formed on the soup, slowly pour the mixture through the sieve into a clean pan (all the skin and impurities, including the egg white film, will be left behind in the sieve); drain about 15 minutes.

Assembly. Gently reheat the soup when ready to serve. Add the white pepper and ladle into warmed serving bowls. Garnish each bowl with a jumble of the julienned crepes.

Bread Salad

Yield: 6 servings

This a rustic, country-style salad in which the croutons are the stars. The 3-minute resting time is very important because it allows the croutons to absorb a little dressing and become slightly soft on the outside yet crunchy on the inside. (Otherwise, the croutons can be rock hard and difficult to eat.) Test one crouton to see how fast it soaks up the dressing before you mix up the whole concoction, because you don't want completely soggy croutons. Different breads take different times to reach the desired saturation point. Correct timing is imperative with this dish!

Dressing
2 tablespoons balsamic vinegar
2 tablespoons Dijon-style mustard
1/2 large egg yolk
2 tablespoons white wine
1 small clove garlic, minced
1/4 teaspoon salt
Freshly ground black pepper
1/2 cup extra virgin olive oil
1/4 small red onion, halved and sliced lengthwise
  into thin julienne

Croutons
1/4 cup olive oil
2 tablespoons unsalted butter
5 cups 1-inch cubes slightly stale crustless French
  or Italian bread
Salt and freshly ground black pepper to taste

Salad
4 cups (about 4 ounces) loosely
  packed mixed baby greens
4 cups watercress, leaves and tender stems
1 small head radicchio, outer leaves
  removed, shredded

Dressing. In a blender or food processor, combine all the ingredients except the olive oil and red onion and process until smooth. With the motor running, add the oil in a thin, steady stream until the dressing is completely emulsified. Transfer to a jar, add the red onion, and refrigerate until ready to use.

Croutons. In a very large nonstick skillet, heat the olive oil and butter over medium-high heat. Add the bread cubes and sauté, shaking the pan and turning the cubes with tongs, until they are golden on all sides. (If you do not have a very large skillet, brown the cubes in 2 batches.) Transfer to a paper towel–lined plate, sprinkle with salt and pepper, and set aside until ready to serve, up to 45 minutes.

Salad. In a very large, chilled mixing bowl, combine the croutons, greens, watercress, and radicchio. Add enough dressing to coat the salad, and toss gently. Let rest for 3 minutes, then taste and adjust the salt and pepper if necessary, and toss again. Divide the salad among 6 chilled salad plates, mounding it high, and serve immediately.

Hong Kong to L.A. Chicken Salad

Yield: 6 servings

This is and isn't a Chinese chicken salad. It's a salad that emerged after I lived in L.A. for a few years. The vinaigrette in this recipe is extremely versatile and, in spite of the long list of ingredients, once you make it, I think you'll use it again (but not necessarily on a salad!). The recipe makes about 2 cups, which is more than enough for 2 pounds of grilled chicken or the Salmon Tempura (page 70).

The Barbecue Sauce provides a wonderful rich, smoky contrast to the lightness of the salad. If you don't want to make it from scratch, feel free to substitute a good-quality store-bought barbecue sauce.

Vinaigrette
1 large egg
2 teaspoons grated fresh ginger
1 clove garlic, finely chopped
**2 tablespoons powdered Japanese mustard or
 1 tablespoon Colman's hot mustard powder**
2 tablespoons soy sauce
2 tablespoons honey
$^1/_2$ cup unseasoned rice vinegar
$^3/_4$ cup peanut oil
$^1/_4$ cup sesame oil

Salad
**1 head Napa cabbage, cored and cut into
 $^1/_4$-inch julienne**
**4 shiitake mushrooms, stems discarded, caps
 cut into $^1/_4$-inch julienne**
**3 whole green onions, sliced $^1/_4$ inch thick on
 the diagonal**
**1 red bell pepper, stemmed, seeded, and cut into
 $^1/_4$-inch julienne**
$^1/_2$ cup soy bean sprouts

Chicken
6 boneless chicken breasts
Salt and freshly ground black pepper to taste
1 tablespoon vegetable oil

Garnish
Vegetable oil for deep-frying
8 wonton wrappers, cut into $1^1/_2$ x $^1/_2$-inch strips
6 whole radicchio leaves, optional
2 tablespoons Barbecue Sauce (page 192)

Vinaigrette. In a blender, combine the egg, ginger, garlic, mustard powder, soy sauce, honey, and vinegar and blend until smooth. Combine the peanut oil and sesame oil in a small bowl. With the motor running, add the oils in a slow, thin stream. Blend for a few seconds more, until the dressing is emulsified, and set aside. The vinaigrette can be made ahead and refrigerated for up to 1 day.

Salad. In a large mixing bowl, combine all the ingredients for the salad and gently toss.

Chicken. Season the chicken breasts with salt and pepper. Heat a large, heavy skillet over medium-high heat and add the vegetable oil. Add the chicken breasts and sauté for 3 to 4 minutes on each side, or until cooked through and no trace of pink remains. Transfer to a cutting board, let rest for 5 minutes, then cut each breast on the diagonal into $^1/_2$-inch-thick slices.

Garnish. In a large, heavy skillet or deep-fryer, heat 2 inches of vegetable oil to 375°. Add the wonton strips and fry for 60 seconds, or until crisp and golden. Remove with a skimmer and drain the strips on a paper towel–lined plate.

Assembly. Toss the salad with enough of the vinaigrette to just coat the leaves. Place 1 radicchio leaf on each serving plate and fill the leaves with a mound of salad. Make a generous pool of the remaining vinaigrette to the side of the salad and place a chicken breast over the vinaigrette, fanning out the slices. Garnish with the fried wonton strips and drizzle the chicken with the Barbecue Sauce. Serve immediately.

German Potato Salad

Yield: 6 servings

In Germany, we use big tin tubs to cool off beer kegs for parties. Sometimes, when I need a lot of this potato salad, I make it in these huge tubs—now that's a lot of potatoes to peel!

Potatoes
12 Red Bee or small red potatoes (golf ball–sized), washed and cut into eighths
1/3 cup extra virgin olive oil
1 tablespoon finely chopped fresh rosemary
3 cloves garlic, finely chopped
1 teaspoon coarse sea salt
1 teaspoon cracked black pepper

Dressing
1/2 cup mayonnaise
3 green onions, green parts only, sliced 1/8 inch thick on the diagonal
2 ribs celery, finely diced
2 thin slices red onion, finely diced
2 tablespoons whole-grain mustard
1 tablespoon red wine vinegar

Potatoes. Preheat the oven to 350°. In a large mixing bowl, combine the potatoes, olive oil, rosemary, garlic, salt, and black pepper and toss to coat well. Transfer the potatoes to a large baking sheet and roast in the oven until they are tender but not mushy, about 45 minutes. Set aside to cool for about 10 minutes.

Dressing. In a small bowl, mix together the mayonnaise, green onions, celery, red onion, mustard, and red wine vinegar. Taste and adjust the seasonings as necessary.

Assembly. Toss the slightly warm potatoes with the dressing until they are evenly coated, then serve immediately. The salad keeps well for 2 days in the refrigerator.

Warm Sweetbread Salad with Walnuts and Tomato Sorbet

Yield: 6 servings

A classic Röckenwagner dish, this salad reflects my belief in the importance of always contrasting flavors, colors, and textures. In this recipe, I'm matching the rich sweetbreads with the tart greens. I often add basil leaves to my greens because they add an earthy fullness to the mix.

Sweetbreads

1 to 2½ teaspoons salt

4 veal sweetbreads (about 5 ounces each before cleaning)

1 tablespoon vegetable oil

¾ cup walnut halves

Dressing

¼ teaspoon salt

Freshly ground black pepper

2 tablespoons balsamic vinegar

6 tablespoons extra virgin olive oil

Salad

6 cups (about 6 ounces) loosely packed mixed greens (such as mâche, arugula, and endive), one-third cut into fine chiffonade

1 recipe Tomato Sorbet (page 198)

⅔ cup sour cream, for garnish

6 sprigs fresh basil, for garnish

Whole red and yellow cherry tomatoes, for garnish

Sweetbreads. Fill a large bowl with ice water and ice cubes and add ¾ teaspoon of the salt. Soak the sweetbreads in the water for 2 hours, changing the water 2 or 3 times, or whenever it becomes cloudy, and adding more ice cubes as needed. Drain the sweetbreads and place them in a large saucepan, cover with fresh cold water, and bring to a boil. Remove the pan from the heat, drain, and shock the sweetbreads in fresh ice water for 5 minutes to stop the cooking. Peel off most of the outer membranes and separate the sweetbreads into smaller, walnut-sized pieces. Spread them out on a paper towel and let dry completely.

Heat a heavy skillet over high heat and when very hot, add the vegetable oil. Add the sweetbreads and sauté for 2 to 3 minutes on each side, or until crispy and golden, then add the walnut pieces and sauté for 1 minute more. Remove the pan from the heat.

Dressing. In a small bowl, whisk together the salt, pepper, and vinegar. Add the oil in a thin stream, whisking until the dressing emulsifies.

Salad. In a large mixing bowl, toss the whole greens with half of the dressing. In a separate bowl, toss the chiffonade of greens with the remaining dressing.

Assembly. Divide the whole greens among 6 serving plates. Mound the chiffonade on top and place a small scoop of the tomato sorbet in the center. Scatter the sweetbreads and walnut pieces around the edges of the salad. Garnish each scoop of sorbet with a dollop of sour cream, a sprig of basil, and a few of the cherry tomatoes.

Salad of Arugula and Sea Scallops with Salmon Caviar Beurre Blanc

Yield: 6 servings

Here's another classic from our early days that I would never dream of taking off the menu. If you can get the presentation right, so guests can lift off the egg as described below, the luscious sauce comes cascading out of the eggshell and it becomes an interactive dish. Combining mashed potatoes and salad may seem unusual, but this dish really does work well.

Scallops

Salt and freshly ground black pepper

10 extra-large sea scallops, sliced into ¹⁄₈-inch-thick medallions (4 to 5 slices per scallop)

Eggshells

6 large eggs

Beurre Blanc

2 tablespoons finely sliced shallots

1 cup dry white wine

¹⁄₂ cup heavy cream

³⁄₄ cup cold unsalted butter, cut into ¹⁄₂-inch cubes

¹⁄₄ teaspoon salt

Freshly ground white pepper

1 to 2 teaspoons freshly squeezed lemon juice

Dash of Tabasco sauce

Salad

1 russet potato, peeled

6 cups (about 6 ounces) loosely packed baby arugula leaves

³⁄₄ cup Balsamic Vinaigrette (see page 193)

4 cups (about 4 ounces) loosely packed mixed baby greens, finely shredded

2 tablespoons salmon caviar

1 tablespoon finely chopped chives

Scallops. Cut six 6 x 6-inch pieces of aluminum foil and brush each with softened butter. Sprinkle with salt and pepper. Make a large circle, leaving a hole in the middle, by overlapping 7 scallop slices on each square. Refrigerate until ready to assemble the salad.

Eggshells. Cut a ¹⁄₂-inch-diameter hole in the pointed end of each egg by sawing gently back and forth with a serrated knife. Empty out the raw eggs into a bowl and save for another use. Carefully rinse the empty eggshells and shake them dry. Set aside.

Beurre Blanc. In a medium, heavy saucepan combine the shallots and white wine and, over medium-high heat, reduce until only a few tablespoons of liquid remain. Add the cream and reduce again by half, then decrease the heat to very low and begin whisking in the cubes of butter a few at a time, waiting until the mixture has emulsified after each addition before adding more. Do not let the sauce boil. (The sauce should be kept warm enough to slowly melt the butter but not hot enough to become oily.) If the sauce gets too hot, remove it from the heat and whisk until it cools slightly. Continue whisking and, when the last piece of butter has been added and the sauce is about to emulsify for the final time, remove the pan from the heat. Whisk in the salt, white pepper, lemon juice, and Tabasco. Set aside until ready to serve, but not longer than 20 minutes.

Salad. Slice the potato into ³/₄-inch-thick pieces. Bring a saucepan of water to a boil and add the potato pieces. Preheat the oven to warm. Boil for 20 minutes, then drain and transfer to a lightly oiled baking sheet. Place the baking sheet in the oven and dry the potato slices for 5 minutes. Transfer the slices to a small mixing bowl and finely mash.

In a separate mixing bowl, toss the arugula with ¹/₂ cup of the vinaigrette. In another bowl, toss the shredded baby greens with the remaining ¹/₄ cup vinaigrette.

Assembly. On each of 6 serving plates, make a ring of arugula leaves around the edge and place a mound of the baby greens in the center. Place a small mound of mashed potato in the center (to hold the egg).

Preheat a grill or grill pan to very high heat and assemble all the ingredients needed to serve the salad. Place the foil squares with the scallop circles directly on the hot grill and cook for 1 minute, repeating until all squares of scallops are seared. Invert the scallop circles over the greens so that the mashed potato is visible through the hole in the center.

Whisk the beurre blanc to re-emulsify it, and stir in the salmon caviar and the chives. Using a teaspoon or a demitasse spoon, fill an empty eggshell about three-quarters full with the warm sauce. Invert the eggshell onto the mashed potato so that the shell is upside down and the mashed potato creates a seal that prevents any of the sauce from leaking out. Repeat for the remaining 5 shells. Serve immediately, instructing each guest to lift off the eggshell so that the sauce inside spills over the scallops.

Fama-Style Chicken Salad

Yield: 6 servings

I love beets, but I know many people don't share my affection for them. The sweet, slightly tart beets in this salad have converted many of our guests into beet lovers. The walnuts alone make a great snack, too.

Dressing

¹/₃ cup mayonnaise

2 teaspoons distilled white vinegar

2 tablespoons Dijon-style mustard

¹/₂ teaspoon salt

Freshly ground black pepper

Dash of Tabasco sauce

¹/₂ cup milk

Beet Salad

4 beets

¹/₄ large yellow onion, finely chopped

¹/₄ cup extra virgin olive oil

2¹/₂ tablespoons red wine vinegar

1 teaspoon sugar

¹/₄ teaspoon salt

Freshly ground black pepper to taste

Spiced Walnuts

2 teaspoons vegetable oil

1¹/₂ cups walnut halves

2 tablespoons confectioners sugar

2 tablespoons curry powder

Chicken Salad

1 tablespoon olive oil

6 boneless, skinless chicken breasts

¹/₄ cup Basil Pesto (page 196), thinned
with 1 tablespoon extra virgin olive oil

2 heads Boston lettuce, pale inner leaves only,
washed, dried, and torn into bite-sized pieces

2 heads romaine lettuce, pale inner leaves only,
washed, dried, and torn into bite-sized pieces

Dressing. Combine all the ingredients and whisk until smooth, adding only enough milk to achieve a creamy consistency. Cover and refrigerate until ready to serve. The dressing can be made up to 1 day ahead.

Beet Salad. In a large saucepan, bring a generous amount of water to a boil and add the beets. Lower the heat to medium and simmer the beets for approximately 35 minutes, or until tender. Transfer them to a bowl of cold water and, when cool, remove and discard the skin. Cut the beets into ¹/₂-inch cubes. In a medium mixing bowl, combine them with the onion, olive oil, vinegar, sugar, salt, and pepper. Toss well, cover, and marinate in the refrigerator for at least 3 hours and up to 4 days, tossing occasionally to redistribute the dressing.

Walnuts. Preheat the broiler to high heat. In a small nonstick skillet, heat the vegetable oil over medium heat and add the walnuts. Stir for about 1 minute, then remove and drain on paper towels, patting the pieces dry. Transfer the walnuts to a baking sheet and spread them out evenly. Combine the confectioners sugar and curry powder in a sifter and sift evenly over the nuts. Place the baking sheet under the hot broiler and toast, watching very carefully and shaking the pan every few seconds. Remove from the broiler when the nuts are lightly toasted. When the nuts are cool, coarsely chop them and set aside. The nuts can be made up to 1 week ahead and stored in an airtight container.

Chicken Salad. Heat a large skillet over medium-high heat and add the olive oil. Add the chicken breasts and sauté until firm, about 4 minutes on each side. (Be careful not to overcook; without the skin to protect them, chicken breasts can dry out easily.) Transfer the chicken breasts to a cutting board and slice thinly against the grain. Brush the slices generously with the Pesto Sauce.

Assembly. In a large mixing bowl, toss the greens with just enough of the dressing to coat them evenly. Place a mound of the dressed greens in the center of each of 6 serving plates, then top the greens with one of the sliced chicken breasts. Arrange 3 small mounds of beet salad around the edges of each plate and scatter the spiced walnuts over the chicken breasts.

Röckenwagner's Coleslaw

Yield: 8 servings

Red cabbage heightens the flavor and color of this coleslaw, but more white cabbage can be substituted.

Dressing
2 teaspoons all-purpose flour
Scant 2 teaspoons dry mustard powder
¼ cup plus 1 tablespoon sugar
Pinch of ground cayenne pepper
1 heaping teaspoon salt
⅔ cup apple cider vinegar
⅔ cup heavy cream
2 large egg yolks
1 tablespoon caraway seeds
1½ tablespoons prepared horseradish

Coleslaw
6 cups (about 1¼ pounds) finely sliced
    white cabbage
1 carrot, grated
1¾ cups (about ½ pound) red cabbage, sliced
    very fine, optional

Dressing. In the top of a double boiler, off the heat, combine the flour, mustard powder, sugar, cayenne, and salt. Bring about 1 inch of water to a simmer in the bottom of the double boiler. In a small saucepan, combine the vinegar and cream and bring to a boil over high heat. Whisk the hot vinegar mixture into the dry ingredients, then place the top of the double boiler over the simmering water. Whisk in the egg yolks and stir until the mixture thickens slightly, about 3 to 4 minutes. Remove from the heat and stir in the caraway seeds and horseradish. Cool to room temperature, cover, and refrigerate until chilled.

Coleslaw. In a large serving bowl, combine vegetables and dressing and toss to mix well. Taste and adjust the seasonings as necessary. Serve immediately or store covered in the refrigerator for up to 2 days.

Arugula, Belgian Endive, and Roasted Beet Salad with Citrus Vinaigrette and Toasted Walnuts

Yield: 4 servings

I developed this recipe for Food & Wine, *when the editors asked me to create a few recipes that contained only 10 grams of fat. This light salad is perfect for fall, and the vinaigrette is marvelous: it's brightly colored, clean-tasting, and has an interesting texture. I usually use a mild olive oil so that the freshness of the citrus flavors isn't overpowered. The sweet soy sauce can be found at Asian markets.*

Roasted Beets

3 beets

1 shallot, finely chopped

2 tablespoons balsamic vinegar

3 tablespoons extra virgin olive oil

Salt and freshly ground black pepper to taste

Citrus Vinaigrette

1 orange, sectioned and juices reserved (page 203)

$^1/_2$ pink grapefruit, sectioned and juices reserved (page 203)

$^1/_2$ lemon, sectioned and juices reserved (page 203)

$^1/_2$ lime, sectioned and juices reserved (page 203)

$^1/_2$ tablespoon sweet soy sauce, or $^1/_2$ teaspoon regular soy sauce whisked with 1 teaspoon sugar

$^1/_2$ teaspoon coriander seeds

$^1/_4$ cup extra virgin olive oil

$^1/_4$ teaspoon salt

Pinch of freshly ground white pepper

8 walnut halves

4 Belgian endives, brown outer leaves removed

3 cups (about 3 ounces) loosely packed baby arugula leaves, rinsed and dried

2 tablespoons finely grated ricotta salata, optional

Beets. Preheat the oven to 350°. Trim the greens and tails from the beets, but do not peel. Wrap them in foil and bake for 35 to 45 minutes, or until tender when pierced with the tip of a knife.

When cool enough to handle, peel the beets and then cut them into $^1/_2$-inch cubes. In a medium bowl, whisk together the shallot, balsamic vinegar, olive oil, and salt and pepper. Add the beet cubes and toss to coat. Allow the mixture to marinate, stirring every 10 minutes, for at least 30 minutes. Cover and refrigerate until ready to serve. (The beets can be prepared 1 day ahead.)

Vinaigrette. In a blender, combine the citrus sections and juices, soy sauce, and coriander seeds. Blend on medium until the mixture is a smooth purée. With the blender running, add the olive oil in a thin stream, blending until the vinaigrette is completely emulsified. Add the salt and white pepper, blend again briefly, and taste for seasoning. Strain the mixture through a coarse sieve to remove any citrus pulp and bits of coriander seeds. Cover and refrigerate until ready to serve.

Assembly. Preheat the oven to 350°. Place the walnut halves on a baking sheet and toast for 8 to 10 minutes, or until the oils are released and the nuts are fragrant but not browned. Set aside.

Separate the leaves of the endive and cut each crosswise into two (three if they are large) 2-inch lengths. Place the endive pieces and arugula in a large bowl and toss to combine. Add $^1/_2$ cup vinaigrette and toss to generously coat the leaves (add more if needed), reserving the remaining vinaigrette for another use. Add the ricotta salata and toss again to distribute evenly.

Divide the greens among 4 large salad plates, piling them high in the center. Surround the greens with the beets and top each salad with 2 walnut halves. Serve immediately.

Pasta Salad with Warm Roasted Eggplant and Home-Cured Tomatoes

Yield: 8 servings

I developed this popular dish for the original lunch menu at Fama. The macaroni shouldn't be too hot when you add the mozzarella or the cheese will get mushy. The salad should showcase the beautifully roasted cubes of eggplant and savory home-cured tomatoes; the mozzarella is not the star of the show. If fresh sage is easily available, by all means add a little chiffonade—it gives the salad another level of flavor.

Roasted Eggplant

1 small eggplant, sliced ¼ inch thick crosswise

Olive oil for brushing

Salt and freshly ground pepper

Salad

1 pound elbow macaroni

24 Home-Cured Tomatoes, cut in half (page 186)

25 basil leaves, coarsely chopped

4 tablespoons balsamic vinegar

6 plum tomatoes, peeled, seeded, and cut into
   ¼-inch dice (page 202)

½ teaspoon salt

Freshly ground black pepper to taste

1 pound fresh mozzarella, cut into ½-inch cubes

⅓ cup extra virgin olive oil

Freshly grated Parmesan for sprinkling

4 fresh sage leaves, cut into
   very fine chiffonade, for garnish

Roasted Eggplant. Preheat the oven to 325°. Lay the eggplant slices on a baking sheet, brush them lightly with the olive oil, and sprinkle with salt and pepper. Turn over, and brush and sprinkle the other side. Roast in the oven for 10 to 15 minutes, or until just golden (do not allow to brown). Remove from the oven, cool slightly, and cut into ¼-inch dice. Set aside.

Salad. Fill a large metal bowl with hot water and set aside to warm. Bring a large stockpot of salted water to a boil. Add the macaroni, cook until al dente, and drain well. Empty the water from the bowl and dry it, then transfer the macaroni to the warmed bowl. Add the eggplant, home-cured tomatoes, basil, balsamic vinegar, diced tomatoes, salt, and pepper. Toss the mixture with a wooden spoon. Immediately add the mozzarella and olive oil, and toss to mix. Taste and adjust the seasonings as necessary. Sprinkle with the Parmesan and sage and serve immediately.

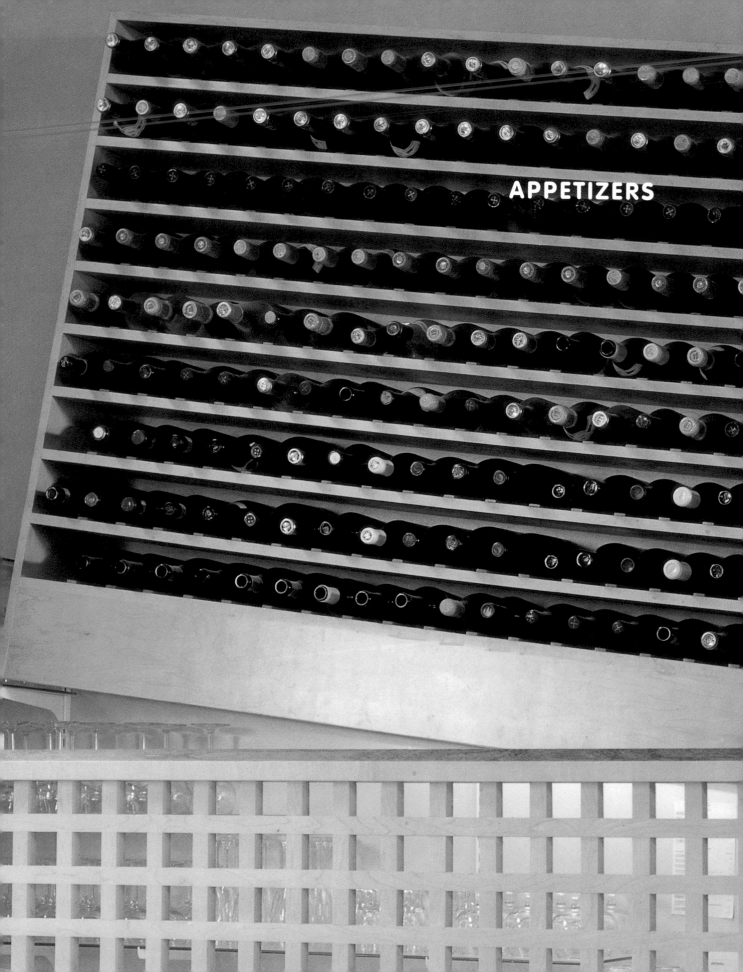

APPETIZERS

Short Stack of Waffle Chips Layered with Smoked Wild Scottish Salmon, Crème Fraîche, and Caviar

Yield: 6 servings

You will need to exert quite a bit of pressure on the potato as you swipe it across the cutting blade of the mandoline, also rotating it 45 degrees each time to get a nice waffle-cut chip. If you don't have a mandoline, try cutting paper-thin slices of potato with a very sharp knife, but the results will not be quite the same.

In a pinch, you could use high-quality store-bought ridged potato chips instead of making your own. You could also substitute salmon caviar for the Tobiko if absolutely necessary, but remember it is saltier than Tobiko and adjust the seasoning accordingly.

▶ Waffle Chips
1 large russet potato
Vegetable oil for deep-frying

Tobiko Vinaigrette
6 hard-boiled egg whites, finely chopped
¼ cup Balsamic Vinaigrette (page 193)
1½ tablespoons Tobiko, salmon, or golden
 whitefish caviar
2 tablespoons finely chopped chives

½ cup crème fraîche
6 ounces smoked wild Scottish or other salmon,
 cut into 1 x 2-inch strips
2 tablespoons Tobiko caviar
12 spears of Belgian endive, bases trimmed
3 cups (about 3 ounces) loosely packed
 mixed baby greens
3 tablespoons Balsamic Vinaigrette (page 193)
2 tablespoons finely chopped chives

Chips. Peel the potato. Using a mandoline on the "gaufrettes" (waffle pattern) setting, thinly slice the potato crosswise into 24 slices about the same size. Fill a large mixing bowl with cold water and rinse the slices, then pat them dry thoroughly with kitchen towels.

In a large, heavy saucepan or deep-fryer, heat about 3 inches of oil to 375° and fry the potato slices 6 at a time, preventing them from overlapping or sticking to each other. They will take 2 to 3 minutes to become golden brown and crisp. With a skimmer or kitchen tongs, transfer the chips to a paper towel–lined baking sheet to drain. Let the oil return to 375°, then repeat with the remaining potato slices.

Vinaigrette. In a medium bowl, gently mix all the ingredients together, taking care not to break up the delicate fish eggs. Refrigerate until ready to serve (not more than 2 hours).

Assembly. Spoon about 2 tablespoons of the Tobiko vinaigrette on one half of each of 6 serving plates. Spread it into a flat circle.

Place all 24 of the potato chips on the work surface. Spoon 1 teaspoon of crème fraîche in a line down the center of each potato chip and top with a few strips of smoked salmon. Place a potato chip on each plate opposite the vinaigrette and top it with another chip placed perpendicular to the first. Continue stacking the potato chips until each plate has 4 criss-crossed layers. Top each stack with 1 teaspoon of the caviar. Place 2 spears of Belgian endive on each plate in a "V" shape with the bases against the side of the stack (near the vinaigrette). Quickly toss the mixed greens with the balsamic vinaigrette in a mixing bowl and place a small mound at the base of each "V." Sprinkle the edge of each plate with a few chives and serve immediately.

Tuna Tartare

Yield: 6 servings

You can serve this tuna tartare without the chips, as it has a lovely fresh flavor of its own. But if you do, you'll miss out on the crunchy texture I love in this dish. I often adjust the amount of hot mustard by adding a little more to the dressing. When passing these as an hors d'oeuvre at parties, I prefer them spicier; when serving several as an appetizer, I tone down the spicy mustard flavor.

Tuna Tartare

$3/4$ pound sushi-quality Ahi tuna, cut into $1/8$-inch dice with a very sharp knife

2 shallots, finely chopped

2 tablespoons finely chopped chives

$1/4$ cup Honey-Mustard Dressing (page 193)

$1/2$ teaspoon salt

$1/2$ teaspoon freshly ground black pepper

2 recipes Waffle Chips (page 46)

$4^1/2$ cups (about 4 ounces) loosely packed mixed baby greens

Scant $1/4$ cup Balsamic Vinaigrette (page 193)

Tartare. In a medium bowl, toss together the tuna, shallots, chives, dressing, salt, and black pepper. (The tuna should be served immediately, but, if necessary, it can be covered and refrigerated for up to $1/2$ hour.)

Assembly. Place 6 chips around the rim of 6 large appetizer plates and mound about 2 teaspoons of the tartare mixture on top of each chip. In a mixing bowl, quickly toss the greens with the vinaigrette and place a mound of greens in the center of each plate. Serve immediately.

Shrimp Cocktail with Bloody Mary Sorbet and Emerald Juice

Yield: 6 servings

This is one of the dishes using fruit and vegetable juices in a series that I developed for a magazine on lowfat cooking. It is a knockout—a fun dish for summer entertaining, when the tomatoes are juicy and full of flavor. No one will expect the icy mound of sorbet in the martini glass. If you can't find the Hansen's mixed greens juice, ask a friend with a juice extractor to make you a little celery and arugula juice. I like to serve this "cocktail" with crisp breadsticks.

6 ribs celery, with leaves attached

$2^1/2$ cups Tomato Sorbet, made with 2 dashes Tabasco sauce (page 198)

6 tablespoons Hansen's mixed greens juice

Dash of vermouth, optional

18 extra-large cooked shrimp, with tail shells

2 tablespoons sour cream or crème fraîche

$1/2$ small bunch chives, cut into $1^1/2$-inch lengths, for garnish

6 sprigs cilantro, for garnish

Assembly. Trim the bottoms of the celery ribs so that they will extend 4 inches above the rim of the glass. Divide the sorbet among 6 martini glasses. Place 1 celery rib upright in the sorbet in each glass. Drizzle 1 tablespoon of the mixed greens juice around the edge of each glass and add a splash of vermouth. Hang 3 shrimp, tail ends outward, over the rim of each glass. Place 1 teaspoon of sour cream in the center of the sorbet, and garnish with several lengths of chive and a sprig of cilantro. Serve immediately.

White Asparagus with Tuna Carpaccio and Ginger Remoulade

Yield: 6 servings

White asparagus has become very popular in recent years, even though its season is limited to 7 or 8 weeks in the springtime. At my parents' restaurant, we often featured white asparagus in an appetizer, main course, soup, omelette, sorbet—whatever we could make with it. All over southern Germany there are restaurants that specialize in, and some that serve nothing but, white asparagus during the season.

The flavor and texture of white asparagus is very different than that of the more common green varieties. In fact, it is sort of watery and can be slightly stringy. There is a very thin membrane on the spear that can taste bitter if it is not carefully peeled away. It may take a little time to get used to white asparagus, but once you have tasted a good one you will understand why such a hoopla is made over this vegetable. Don't even consider using the canned variety. If fresh white asparagus is unavailable, substitute green asparagus and omit the lemon juice, sugar, and butter from the cooking water.

▶ Remoulade

¹/₄ cup finely chopped gherkins (about 3 large)

1¹/₂ tablespoons capers, rinsed and drained

1 large shallot, finely chopped

³/₄ cup loosely packed flat-leaf parsley, finely chopped

2 teaspoons grated fresh ginger

¹/₄ teaspoon salt

¹/₄ teaspoon freshly ground black pepper

¹/₄ teaspoon Tabasco sauce

¹/₂ cup mayonnaise

continued

Crisp Foie Gras Wontons with Spicy Plum Wine Sauce

Yield: 6 servings

For these ravioli, we deep-fry wonton skins to create a very special texture and contrast to the creamy foie gras. Foie gras can be frozen, which is handy since it's virtually impossible to buy less than a whole liver. Be sure to avoid using canned foie gras, which has an unappetizing texture and flavor.

▶ Ravioli

**¹/₂ pound fresh or frozen foie gras, sliced
¹/₂ inch thick**

1 tablespoon unsalted butter

1 shallot, finely chopped

1 clove garlic, finely chopped

3 cups (about 6 ounces) shiitake mushroom caps, cut into ¹/₄-inch dice

¹/₂ teaspoon salt

¹/₄ teaspoon freshly ground black pepper

18 fresh wonton wrappers

Vegetable oil for deep-frying

2 cups frisée leaves

¹/₄ cup Balsamic Vinaigrette (page 193)

1¹/₂ cups Spicy Plum Wine Sauce (page 99)

Ravioli. Heat a heavy, well-seasoned cast iron skillet over high heat until it is very hot. Add the slices of foie gras and sear in the dry pan for 20 seconds on each side. Transfer to a cutting board, leaving the juices in the pan, cool for 5 minutes, and then cut into ¹/₄-inch dice.

Heat the same pan over medium-high heat and add the butter to the foie gras juices. Add the shallot and garlic and sauté, stirring occasionally, for 3 to 4 minutes, or until tender. Add the mushroom caps and continue cooking for about 5 minutes, or until the mushrooms have given up their liquid and the mixture is quite dry. Stir in the salt and pepper and set aside.

On a lightly floured cutting board, lay a wonton wrapper and brush all four edges with water. Put a generous teaspoon of the mushroom mixture in the center, top with 4 or 5 cubes of foie gras, and lift 2 of the opposite corners to meet in the center. Press the very tips together firmly, then lift the remaining 2 corners and press together at the top, forming a tall package. Press all the seams and corners together very firmly to seal. There should be no air holes. Repeat with the remaining wonton wrappers. (The ravioli can be covered and refrigerated for up to 3 hours before frying.)

In a large, heavy saucepan or deep-fryer, heat about 4 inches of vegetable oil to 375°. Deep-fry the ravioli, in batches if necessary, for about 2 minutes, turning them over after 1 minute. Remove with a skimmer and drain on paper towels. Repeat with the remaining ravioli, allowing the oil to return to 375° before frying each batch.

Assembly. Toss the frisée with the vinaigrette and mound some of the leaves in the center of each of 6 heated shallow bowls. Place 3 ravioli around the edges of the salad, and spoon about ¹/₄ cup of the plum sauce in the bottom of the bowls. Serve immediately.

Marinated Shiitake Mushrooms Wrapped in Rice Paper

Yield: 6 servings

The marinated mushrooms are great in this dish. They also make a wonderful snack, so if you don't want to cook the whole dish, just make the mushrooms. Do try to find the small, bite-sized shiitakes, because they are really tender and cook quickly. This dish is also nice as part of an hors d'oeuvres platter. Or, instead of 4 servings, serve 3 sections per person as a lighter first course. The mushrooms take some time to marinate, so be sure to plan ahead. You can find the Sambal Olek and shizo or oba leaves at an Asian market.

Marinated Shiitake Mushrooms

2 teaspoons sesame oil

1 teaspoon sliced garlic

1 tablespoon sliced fresh ginger

3/4 pound baby shiitake mushroom caps (smaller than 1 1/2 inches in diameter), wiped clean and stems removed

1 cup rice vinegar

1 teaspoon Sambal Olek chili paste

1/2 teaspoon salt

1/2 cup Sesame Vinaigrette (page 65)

Rice Paper Rolls

6 sheets rice paper

18 shizo or oba leaves

4 ounces enoki mushrooms, bottom two-thirds discarded

1 1/2 cups daikon sprouts

3 cups Daikon, Carrot, and Cucumber Salad (page 70)

1/2 cup Honey-Mustard Dressing (page 193)

Mushrooms. In a large, heavy saucepan, heat the sesame oil over medium heat. Add the garlic, ginger, and mushrooms and sauté for 3 minutes, or until the mushrooms are just seared and still dry. Deglaze the pan with the vinegar and reduce over medium-high heat until almost no liquid remains. Stir in the chili paste and salt and remove from the heat. Add the vinaigrette and stir to mix. Set aside and allow to marinate for at least 6 hours. (The marinated mushrooms can be kept covered in the refrigerator for up to 4 days.)

Rolls. Fill a large bowl or skillet with lukewarm water and assemble all of the ingredients for the rolls on the work surface. Working with one sheet at a time, dip the rice paper into the warm water for about 8 seconds, remove it, shake off the excess water, and transfer it to the work surface. (The paper should be very pliable.) Working quickly, lay 3 shizo leaves across the center of the paper, then lay a line of marinated shiitakes over the leaves. Lay some enoki mushrooms and daikon sprouts in a line below the mushrooms, extending all the way across to the sides. Starting from the bottom, tightly roll up the paper, tucking the ends in with your fingers and being careful not to tear it. (The rolls can be covered and set aside, seam sides down, on a wet towel for up to 30 minutes before serving.)

Assembly. Place a mound of Daikon, Carrot, and Cucumber Salad on each of 6 plates. Cut each roll into 4 equal pieces and lean them up against the salad. Spoon a little of the dressing on the side of the plate and serve immediately.

Crab Soufflé with Sliced Mango and Lobster Butter Sauce

Yield: 6 servings

I remember when I made this soufflé for the first time like it was yesterday because it was such a big hit. I had invited just six people to a special dinner at my in-laws', where my wife and I were staying after leaving Le Perroquet in Chicago and moving to L.A. in 1984. The staff at Le Perroquet had been making a lot of dessert soufflés, so I took up the challenge of creating a distinctive savory soufflé. I made the crab stock extra flavorful, and when our guests tasted it that first time, it was clear that it worked perfectly. At that time I hadn't even opened the first restaurant, but when I did, the first thing on the menu was this soufflé. I don't plan to ever strike it from the menu.

Crab Sauce Base

1 tablespoon vegetable oil
2 large yellow onions, peeled and quartered
$^1/_2$ crab, with shell on, coarsely chopped
1 cup tomato juice
$1^1/_2$ tablespoons tomato paste
2 cups water

Soufflé

$1^1/_2$ cups milk
$^1/_4$ cup unsalted butter
$^1/_4$ cup all-purpose flour
5 large egg yolks
1 teaspoon salt
$^1/_2$ teaspoon Tabasco sauce

Lobster Butter Sauce

2 tablespoons vegetable oil
4 shallots, finely chopped
1 clove garlic, finely chopped
1 anchovy fillet, minced
1 teaspoon tomato paste
2 cups Lobster Stock (page 188)
$^1/_3$ cup heavy cream

$^1/_2$ teaspoon salt
$^1/_4$ teaspoon freshly ground black pepper or to taste
Dash of Tabasco sauce
$^1/_2$ teaspoon freshly squeezed lemon juice
1 cup cold unsalted butter, cut into 1/2-inch cubes

7 large egg whites, at room temperature
Pinch of salt
1 bunch baby spinach, leaves only
1 ripe mango, peeled, pitted, and thinly sliced
2 tablespoons pink peppercorns, for garnish

Base. Heat a very large, heavy skillet or Dutch oven over medium-high heat and add the oil. Add the onions and crab pieces and sauté slowly, stirring occasionally with a wooden spoon, until the mixture is deep golden and very crusty, about 15 to 20 minutes. (Regulate the heat so that the mixture sizzles but doesn't burn.) Add the tomato juice, tomato paste, and water and deglaze the pan, stirring and scraping the bottom and sides of the pan to release all the flavorful bits. Bring the mixture to a slow simmer. Simmer partially covered for 30 minutes, or until thickened. Pass through a fine sieve into a clean saucepan, pressing firmly on the solids to extract any remaining liquid. Discard all of the solids. Over medium heat, simmer the strained sauce until reduced to two-thirds of its original volume, a scant 1 cup. Set aside. (If desired, the sauce can be frozen for up to 1 month. Just thaw and bring to room temperature before continuing with the recipe.)

continued

Crab Soufflé *continued*

Soufflé Base. Thoroughly butter the base, sides, and top rim of six 4-ounce ramekins and dust well with flour, shaking out the excess. In a small saucepan, bring the milk to a boil and set it aside. In a medium saucepan, melt the butter over medium heat. When it is foamy, add the flour, remove from the heat and stir the mixture with a wooden spoon until the flour is incorporated and the mixture is a smooth, thick paste. Return the roux to the heat and stir over medium-low heat for about 5 minutes, or until bubbling but not brown. Gradually whisk in the milk until the mixture is smooth, then pour the hot mixture into the bowl of an electric mixer and mix on medium speed. Add the egg yolks 1 at a time, then mix in the salt, Tabasco, and the crab sauce base. (If desired, this mixture can be cooled and refrigerated for up to 2 hours before continuing.)

Sauce. Heat a large saucepan over medium heat and add the vegetable oil. Add the shallots and sauté for 2 to 3 minutes, or until softened. Add the garlic, anchovy, and tomato paste and sauté for 1 minute more. Stir in the lobster stock and regulate the heat so that the liquid comes to a rapid simmer. Reduce to about three-quarters of the original volume, leaving about $1/2$ cup of liquid. Add the cream and reduce again to just less than $1/2$ cup of syrupy liquid. Stir in the salt, pepper, Tabasco, and lemon juice. Decrease the heat to very low and whisk in the butter a few pieces at a time, waiting until they are absorbed before adding more. (Do not let the sauce boil.) Just before the last piece of butter has been absorbed, remove the saucepan from the heat and whisk until smooth. Strain the sauce through a fine sieve into a clean pan, cover, and set aside (not longer than 30 minutes).

Soufflés. Preheat the oven to 400°. Put a kettle of water on to boil for the water bath (bain-marie). In a perfectly clean bowl with clean beaters (any trace of fat will prevent the egg whites from achieving their maximum loft), beat the egg whites and salt to stiff peaks, but not until they are grainy. Stir about one-quarter of the egg whites into the soufflé mixture to loosen it, then carefully fold in the remaining egg whites, making sure the mixture is evenly blended. Take care not to overfold and deflate the egg whites.

Fill the prepared ramekins with the mixture to within $1/8$ inch of the rim, then run a finger around the inside of each rim to free the top of the soufflés from the ramekins and allow them to rise evenly. Place the ramekins in a roasting pan and pour enough boiling water into the pan to come halfway up the sides of the ramekins. Place the pan on the stovetop and bring the water to a simmer. Place the pan in the oven and bake, without opening the door, for 12 to 15 minutes, or until the soufflés have doubled in height.

Assembly. While the soufflés are baking, bring a pan of water to a simmer. Add the spinach leaves and blanch for 15 seconds. Remove with a skimmer, then shock in ice water. Spread the leaves out on paper towels to drain.

Place a few spinach leaves on one side of each of 6 large serving plates. Divide the mango slices among the plates and fan them out over the spinach. Place 1 soufflé opposite the spinach and mango on each plate. Garnish with the peppercorns. Serve immediately, passing the warm lobster sauce at the table.

Kadaifi-Wrapped Shrimp on Eggplant Caviar with Balsamic Tomatoes

Yield: 6 servings

Kadaifi dough is similar to phyllo dough and looks like very fine strands of phyllo bunched together, but it's actually made from a runnier dough that's poured through a fine sieve onto a hot, turning, circular griddle and cooked instantaneously. When using both phyllo and kadaifi, it's important to work very fast and keep it covered with a slightly damp kitchen towel so that it will stay pliable and not become brittle.

Kadaifi is a very versatile product. It is perfect for the home cook because it's ready-made, easy to use, and can be wrapped around almost anything. It adds texture, color, and flavor to any dish.

Shrimp

¼ cup olive oil

2 cloves garlic, finely chopped

1 generous tablespoon basil chiffonade
   (about 4 leaves)

1¼ pounds jumbo shrimp, peeled and deveined

½ pound kadaifi dough, thawed and cut into
   thirty 1½ x 7-inch-long strips

Balsamic Tomatoes

9 plum tomatoes, peeled, seeded,
   and cut into ¼-inch dice

3 tablespoons balsamic vinegar

¼ teaspoon salt

¼ teaspoon freshly ground black pepper

¼ cup extra virgin olive oil

Vegetable oil for deep-frying

1¼ cups Melitzana (page 88)

Shrimp. In a medium bowl, combine the olive oil, garlic, and basil and stir to combine. Add the shrimp, toss to coat well, then marinate, covered, in the refrigerator for 45 minutes. Drain the shrimp and discard the marinade. Unravel a strip of kadaifi dough about 7 inches long and the thickness of your middle finger. Hold the dough against the side of the shrimp with one finger, then twist and wrap the other end around the shrimp in a spiral. Set the shrimp seam side down on a lightly oiled baking sheet and repeat with the remaining shrimp. Cover with a kitchen towel and refrigerate until needed (for up to 1 hour).

Tomatoes. Place the tomatoes, balsamic vinegar, salt, and pepper in a medium mixing bowl and toss to combine. Add the olive oil, adding additional oil if necessary to bind the mixture. Taste and adjust the seasonings if necessary, then set aside.

Assembly. In a large, heavy saucepan or deep-fryer, heat a generous amount of oil to 350°. Add the shrimp, 6 to 8 at a time, and fry until they are golden, about 3 to 4 minutes. Remove with a skimmer and place on a paper towel–lined baking sheet in a warm oven to drain.

Place a large dollop of Melitzana in the center of each of 6 warmed serving plates. Lean 4 of the shrimp up against the Melitzana in a circle. Place about 2 teaspoons of the Balsamic Tomatoes between each shrimp and serve immediately.

Langoustine Purses with Leeks and Ginger in a Port Wine Reduction

Yield: 6 servings

Rice paper is readily available in most Asian markets. When you buy rice paper, make sure that the sheets are not cracked because cracks turn into holes when the paper is wet, making it nearly impossible to work with. Note that the Curry Oil should be made 1 to 2 days ahead.

▶ Port Wine Reduction

4 cups ruby port

2 shallots, thinly sliced

1 piece star anise

¼ cup Veal Stock (page 189)

Langoustine Purses

¼ cup unsalted butter

4 cups coarsely chopped leeks, white and light green parts only (about 2 large leeks)

2 cloves garlic, thinly sliced

2 tablespoons grated fresh ginger

½ cup Lobster Stock (page 188)

½ teaspoon salt

¼ teaspoon freshly ground black pepper

¼ cup basil chiffonade (about 15 leaves)

6 langoustine tails

1½ tablespoons olive oil

18 large spinach leaves

6 (8 x ¼-inch) strips of leek, white and green parts cut from the outer leaves

6 (8-inch) round sheets of rice paper

2 mangoes, peeled, pitted and thinly sliced

2 teaspoons clarified butter (page 202)

1¼ cups Curry Oil (page 200)

Reduction. In a heavy pan over medium heat, combine the port, shallots, and anise. Reduce to about one-fourth of the original volume (this can take up to 1½ hours). Add the veal stock, stir to blend, and reduce again to just less than 1 cup of syrupy liquid. Strain into a clean pan and set aside.

Purses. In a heavy pan over medium-low heat, melt the butter and add the chopped leeks. Sweat for 8 to 10 minutes, or until softened, then add the garlic and ginger and cook for 3 minutes more. Add the lobster stock, increase the heat to medium-high, and reduce until almost no liquid remains. Stir in the salt and pepper and remove from the heat. Stir in the basil, taste for seasoning and set aside to cool.

Season the langoustine tails with salt and pepper. In a very hot skillet, add the olive oil then the tails, searing them briefly for 30 to 45 seconds on each side.

Bring a pan of water to a simmer. Add the whole spinach leaves and blanch for 15 seconds. Remove with a skimmer, then shock in ice water. Spread the leaves out on paper towels to drain. Bring the water in the pan to a boil. Add the leek strips and blanch for 1 minute. Remove with a skimmer, then shock in ice water and drain. Wet a kitchen towel with warm water, squeeze out the excess, and place it on the counter. Place a circle of rice paper on the lower half of the towel and fold over the top half of the towel, enclosing the rice paper. Press down gently, and let rest for 2 minutes. Unfold the towel and transfer the softened rice paper to a work surface. Place 3 blanched spinach leaves in the center of each

continued

Langoustine Purses *continued*

circle, overlapping slightly, and mound 2 table-spoons of the cooled leek mixture in the center. Top with a langoustine tail and another table-spoon of leeks. Lift the sides of the rice paper and gather together at the top. Tie the tops securely with a leek strip. Repeat with the other 5 circles of rice paper. Transfer the purses to the refrigerator until ready to serve.

Preheat the oven to 400°. Brush an ovenproof nonstick pan with the clarified butter. Place the langoustine purses in the pan. Bake the purses for 8 to 10 minutes, or until they are golden and crisp.

Assembly. Warm the reduction until it is thin enough to pour. On each of 6 serving plates, fan out a circle of overlapping mango slices. Place a purse over the mango slices on each plate, and drizzle the Port Wine Reduction and Curry Oil around the edges.

The Stammtisch Table

The origins of the stammtisch table go way, way back. In Germany and Austria, every restaurant and tavern has always had a stammtisch. Usually made out of a big slab of oak, the tables seat 8 to 15 people. Usually, an old copper ashtray sits in the middle supporting a small sign that declares STAMMTISCH, so the table can't be mistaken for anything else. Stammtisches have always been a place for people to gather, to find company and conversation. It's where you'll find a cross-section of the community —the butcher, the baker, the banker, and especially the innkeeper—discussing politics and community affairs, or maybe indulging in a little gossip along with a beer and a snack.

The stammtisch is governed by quite a few rules and traditions. For instance, the regular attendees always sit at the same place. Some stammtisches are even worn where the members' elbows have rested on the tabletop for years and years. Historically, the table was mostly, if not exclusively, a male domain, and one would never go to a stammtisch where he wasn't known without having been invited by another member.

I love that sense of community, of belonging to something. Here in Los Angeles, everyone seems to jump in their cars and speed away without ever talking with anyone. I wanted to counteract that by providing a place for people to get together that wasn't a bar. I wanted to put a contemporary spin on the stammtisch, but I didn't know if the concept would appeal to Los Angelenos. Now that I've nurtured it for several years, educating people about the tradition, the idea has really taken off. Every Tuesday night we have two stammtisches going, one inside and one outside, and then we have to add zillions of chairs to both of them. It's turned into something like a salon, or the old round table from the Algonquin, and become so popular that I have to think about where it should go from here. The group of people who come know they will see their friends and catch up on the news. It's getting a little too big for itself now, and that tells me there's a craving for this kind of informal get-together in our community. At Röckenwagner, the tables have become a modern hybrid, preserving the core of the old German tradition within a looser California setting, where anybody and everybody is welcome.

Spicy Seared Tuna Sashimi with Sesame Vinaigrette

Yield: 6 servings

This is a simple, beautiful dish with fresh flavors. The technique for searing the tuna can be used for salmon or whitefish as well. It is a foolproof way to cook very thin slices of meat or fish without having them fall apart. Be sure that the tuna is still quite pink on the top when you transfer it to the salad. It is certainly worth the effort involved in making the shiitakes, as they will keep for up to 1 week in the refrigerator. If you substitute a different lettuce for the mizuna, endive, or red leaf, choose another sturdy lettuce that can hold up underneath the tuna.

Ginger Butter
2 tablespoons unsalted butter
1 teaspoon minced fresh ginger

Sesame Vinaigrette
¹/₃ cup rice vinegar
1¹/₄ teaspoons granulated sugar
¹/₂ teaspoon salt
¹/₄ teaspoon freshly ground black pepper
¹/₂ tablespoon white sesame seeds,
   toasted (page 203)
1 tablespoon soy sauce
2 tablespoons sesame oil
¹/₄ cup vegetable oil

Salt
Freshly ground white pepper
1¹/₂ pounds sushi-quality Ahi tuna
6 cups (about 6 ounces) loosely packed Mizuna
   greens, curly endive, or red leaf lettuce
1 cup Marinated Shiitake Mushrooms, for
   garnish (page 53)
2 tablespoons finely chopped chives, for garnish

Butter. Melt the butter over low heat, stir in the ginger and remove from the heat. Allow the mixture to infuse for 2 to 3 hours or overnight for the flavor to develop.

Vinaigrette. In a small saucepan, heat the vinegar and whisk in the sugar until it is dissolved. Remove from the heat and allow to cool. Stir in the salt, pepper, sesame seeds, and soy sauce, then whisk in the sesame and vegetable oils, whisking until the mixture is completely emulsified.

Assembly. Reheat the butter and ginger infusion until it is soft enough to spread easily. Brush six 5 x 5-inch squares of aluminum foil with some of this mixture, and sprinkle with salt and white pepper. With a very sharp knife, slice the tuna against the grain about ³/8 inch thick and lay 2 slices in a single layer on each piece of foil. Preheat a grill, grill pan, or large, heavy skillet to very high heat.

Toss the greens with just enough vinaigrette to coat the leaves. Reserve the remaining vinaigrette for another use. Mound an equal amount of the salad on each of 6 serving plates.

Transfer the sheets of foil to the hot grill and cook for about 30 seconds, or until the tuna is seared on one side and still raw on the other. Immediately transfer the tuna slices, raw side up, to the plates, draping them around the edges of the salad. Garnish with the mushrooms and chives and serve immediately.

Crab and Goat Cheese Strudel with Red Bell Pepper Sauce

Yield: 6 servings

I have always had a great affection for strudels. One of my fondest memories is of going to Bavaria—the land of strudel—with my aunt. We went to one restaurant where the main course was apple strudel with vanilla sauce. I was in heaven!

Strudel dough is really quite easy to make, but here I've called for phyllo dough instead, which is easier to use, if not quite authentic. Be sure to cover the phyllo dough with a damp kitchen towel right up to the moment that you begin assembling the strudel. If the dough isn't covered, it will dry out and become too brittle to work with.

▶ Red Bell Pepper Sauce

4 roasted red bell peppers, stemmed, seeded,
   and peeled (page 202)
Juice of $^{1}/_{2}$ lime
$^{1}/_{4}$ cup sour cream
1 teaspoon sweet paprika
$^{1}/_{2}$ teaspoon salt
Freshly ground black pepper to taste

Strudels

$^{1}/_{2}$ cup soft goat cheese, at room temperature
Juice of $^{1}/_{2}$ lemon
$^{1}/_{2}$ teaspoon salt
$^{1}/_{4}$ teaspoon freshly ground black pepper
1 tablespoon finely chopped fresh basil
   (about 4 leaves)
12 small asparagus spears,
   bottom 2 inches of stalk peeled
4 sheets phyllo dough, thawed
$^{1}/_{3}$ cup unsalted clarified butter (page 202)
$^{1}/_{2}$ pound cooked crabmeat,
   picked over and shredded
4 ($^{1}/_{2}$-inch-thick) slices of a large red onion,
   grilled until charred and softened
3 tablespoons fine dry bread crumbs

6 sprigs of fresh basil, for garnish

Sauce. In a blender, process the bell peppers into a smooth purée. You should have about 1 cup of purée. In a medium mixing bowl, combine the red pepper purée with the lime juice, sour cream, paprika, salt, and pepper. Blend well and set aside. (The sauce can be prepared in advance, covered, and refrigerated. Just bring it to room temperature before continuing with the recipe.)

Strudels. In a medium mixing bowl, combine the goat cheese with the lemon juice, salt, pepper, and basil and set aside. Bring a saucepan of water to a boil. Add the asparagus, and blanch for 4 minutes, then shock in ice water and drain.

Trim the phyllo sheets to 12 x 12 inches. Lay one sheet of phyllo on a lightly floured work surface, brush it with a little clarified butter, and place another sheet on top. Set aside and repeat with the remaining two sheets.

Spread half of the goat cheese mixture in a line $1/2$ inch from one long edge of each layered phyllo sheet. Next to the strip, toward the center of the sheet, spoon half of the shredded crabmeat in a long line. Distribute half the grilled onions and asparagus next to the crab, brush the other long edge and the 2 short ends of the phyllo with clarified butter. Starting with the long edge that the filling is closest to, roll up the strudel tightly, squeezing the edges to seal them. Repeat with the second layered sheet of phyllo.

Place the 2 strudels seam side down on a baking sheet and generously brush the outside of each strudel with clarified butter. Sprinkle with the bread crumbs and set aside. (At this point, the strudels can be refrigerated for up to 2 hours. Just bring them to room temperature before continuing with the recipe.)

Preheat the oven to 400°. Bake the strudels in the hot oven for 15 to 20 minutes, or until they are crisp and golden. Transfer them to a cutting board, let rest for 5 minutes, and then slice off and discard (or eat) the ends of the strudels.

Assembly. Slice each strudel into 3 equal lengths and slice each length into 3 rounds. Make a pool of the sauce on each of 6 plates and lay 3 rounds over the sauce. Place a basil leaf atop each round and serve immediately.

Rock Shrimp Samosas with Lemon Chutney

Yield: 45 small samosas

In the last three years I have grown very fond of Indian food. There is a restaurant here in Los Angeles called Nawab of India, which, I am told by native Indians, is one of the most authentic outside of India. I've learned a lot about the food just by dining there. I love the spices, with their heavy aromas, and the breads. I created this version of the traditional Indian samosa to highlight the sweet rock shrimp we enjoy here on the West Coast. These samosas make a great snack, and are really quite simple to prepare.

Filling

1 large russet potato, peeled and cut into
  ¹/₄-inch dice
¹/₂ cup fresh or frozen and thawed green peas
2 tablespoons vegetable oil
6 ounces rock or other small shrimp, cut into
  ¹/₄-inch pieces
¹/₄ white onion, cut into ¹/₄-inch dice
¹/₂ small clove garlic, minced
2 teaspoons good-quality curry powder
2 teaspoons mustard seed
¹/₂ teaspoon ground cumin
¹/₂ teaspoon ground coriander
Pinch of ground cardamom
¹/₂ teaspoon salt
¹/₄ teaspoon freshly ground white pepper

Dough

2¹/₂ cups all-purpose flour
¹/₃ cup soybean oil
1¹/₂ teaspoons salt
²/₃ cup water

Vegetable oil for deep-frying
Lemon Chutney (page 132)
Tzatziki (page 89)

Filling. Bring a medium saucepan of water to a boil. Add the potato cubes and blanch for 8 minutes, then add the peas and blanch for 2 minutes more. Using a skimmer, remove the potatoes and peas and spread them out on paper towels to drain.

Heat a medium skillet over medium-high heat and add the vegetable oil. When the oil is very hot, add the shrimp and onion and toss for 3 to 4 minutes, or until the shrimp are pink and the onion is golden. Add the potatoes and peas and cook for 2 minutes more. Remove from the heat and transfer the mixture to a large mixing bowl. Add the garlic, spices, salt, and white pepper and toss to mix well. Cover and set aside. (The mixture can be refrigerated for up to 4 hours.)

Dough. In the bowl of a food processor, combine the flour, soybean oil, and salt and process until the mixture is flaky. Add the water and process just until the dough comes together, adding another tablespoon of water if necessary. Turn the dough out onto a lightly floured surface and knead until it is smooth and elastic, about 5 minutes. Place the dough in a bowl, brush it with a little soybean oil, and cover it with a kitchen towel to keep it from drying out as you work. (At this stage, the dough can rest at room temperature for up to 4 hours.)

Assembly. Keeping the dough covered with a damp kitchen towel as you work, make 4 samosas at a time. Pinch off 2 pieces of dough, each about the size of a walnut, and roll them with your palm into balls about 1¹/₄ inches in diameter. On a lightly floured surface, roll them out with a rolling pin into 4-inch-diameter circles about ¹/₈ inch thick. Cut each circle in half and brush the rounded edge with a little water. Shape each semicircle into a cone and place a teaspoon of the potato and shrimp mixture deep inside. Moisten the top edges and press them firmly to close. Repeat until you have used all of the dough. Cover the samosas and set aside. (The filled samosas can be stored in the refrigerator for up to 2 hours. Just bring them to room temperature before frying.)

Preheat the oven to 200°. Line 2 large baking sheets with paper towels and place in the oven to warm. In a large, heavy saucepan or deep-fryer, heat about 3 inches of vegetable oil to 375°. Add the samosas, 5 or 6 at a time, and fry until they are golden brown on all sides, about 3 to 4 minutes. Using a skimmer, transfer the samosas to the warm baking sheets. Serve immediately with the Lemon Chutney and Tzatziki.

Salmon Tempura with Daikon Salad

Yield: 6 servings

This is one of our best-selling appetizers. It appeals on every level: visual, textural, and taste. Although it may be a bit time-consuming to make, it is well worth it. When you see how the dish looks and taste it for the first time, I'm sure it will become a permanent recipe in your special-occasion repertoire. You will need a bamboo sushi wrapper to make the rolls. Look for one, along with the nori, black sesame seeds, and shizo or oba leaves, at Asian markets and kitchenware suppliers.

Tempura Batter

1¼ to 1½ cups cold soda water

1 cup all-purpose flour

¼ cup cornstarch

2 teaspoons salt

Salmon Rolls

12 asparagus spears, trimmed and bottom
  2 inches peeled

3 (8 x 8-inch) sheets nori (seaweed)

3 (4 x 8-inch) sheets of fresh salmon, about
  ³/₈ inch thick (see Note)

1 tablespoon black sesame seeds

Salt and freshly ground black pepper

9 shizo or oba leaves

Daikon, Carrot, and Cucumber Salad

¼ pound trimmed daikon radish, cut into
  2 x ⅛-inch julienne

2 carrots, cut into 2 x ⅛-inch julienne

¼ pound English cucumbers, cut into
  2 x ⅛-inch julienne

½ teaspoon salt

Freshly ground black pepper to taste

1 cup Honey-Mustard Dressing (page 193)

Vegetable oil for deep-frying

Daikon radish sprouts, for garnish

Batter. Place 1¼ cups of the soda water in a medium mixing bowl and sift the flour and cornstarch over it. Add the salt and whisk until evenly blended. The batter should be the consistency of thin pancake batter. If necessary, add additional soda water 1 tablespoon at a time. Cover and refrigerate for 45 minutes to 1 hour.

Rolls. Bring a saucepan of water to a boil. Add the asparagus, blanch for 6 minutes, then shock in ice water and drain.

Place a bamboo sushi wrapper on a work surface with the slats crosswise. Center one sheet of nori on the sushi wrapper. Place a sheet of salmon on top of the nori, leaving a 1-inch border of nori uncovered along the top. Sprinkle 1 teaspoon of black sesame seeds evenly over the salmon and season with salt and black pepper. Place 3 shizo leaves equidistant from each other and the edges, then add 4 asparagus spears side by side horizontally about 1 inch above the bottom edge.

Grasping the bamboo mat, the nori, and the edge of the salmon on the bottom, tightly roll up, enclosing the asparagus. Firmly press the 1-inch border at the top to create a seal. (The moisture from the salmon will be enough to make the two pieces of nori adhere to each other.) The roll should be about 1¾ inches in diameter. Carefully remove the bamboo mat, transfer the salmon roll to a plate, and refrigerate. Repeat with the remaining ingredients, making 2 more salmon rolls. (The rolls can be refrigerated for up to 2 hours before continuing with the recipe.)

continued

Salmon Tempura *continued*

With a serrated knife, cut each of the 3 salmon rolls in half crosswise so that you have six 4-inch-long rolls. In a large, heavy saucepan heat 4 inches of vegetable oil to 375°. Insert one long bamboo skewer crosswise through one end of a salmon roll, then insert another skewer through the other end. Using the ends of the skewers as handles, dip the roll into the tempura batter so that it is completely coated, letting the excess batter drip back into the bowl. Carefully immerse the roll in the hot oil, and after 10 seconds, gently push it off the skewers to float free in the oil. Fry for about $1^1/_2$ minutes more, or until the batter is crisp and slightly puffed.

With a skimmer, transfer the first roll to a paper towel–lined plate and keep warm in a very low oven. With the skimmer, remove any leftover bits of batter from the oil, so that they don't burn and smoke. Repeat with the remaining 5 rolls. With a serrated knife, quickly trim off the ends of the rolls and cut each into five $^3/_4$-inch-long rounds.

Salad. In a medium mixing bowl, toss the julienned vegetables with the salt, pepper, and $^1/_2$ cup of the dressing.

Assembly. Make a tall mound of the salad in the center of each of 6 serving plates. Lean 5 tempura rolls against the salad around the base. Dot the remaining $^1/_2$ cup of dressing around the outer edge of each plate. Garnish the salad on each plate with a pinch of daikon sprouts.

Note: Either ask your fishmonger to cut the salmon sheets for you, or buy a fillet of salmon cut from the tail section (where it is the thinnest) and proceed as follows. Make a guide for your knife by placing 2 large wooden chopsticks about 6 inches apart on a cutting board. Place the salmon fillet between them lengthwise and rest the chopsticks against the long edges of the fish. Holding a very long, sharp filleting knife so that one flat side of the blade is parallel to the cutting board, slice the salmon horizontally while steadying the top of the salmon with your other hand. When you have cut one sheet, lift it off the fillet and repeat the process a second and a third time, until you have 3 sheets (the blade may end up resting against the guides). Trim the salmon slices to 4 x 8 inches and reserve the trimmings for another use.

Röckenwagner-Style Oyster Shooters

Yield: 6 servings

This is a very special recipe. The Eucalyptus Honey Vinegar is the essential ingredient—there is no comparable substitute. It's like trying to find a substitute for foie gras or truffles. This little hors d'oeuvre explodes on the palate in a cold, fresh combination of flavors. Oyster shooters are definitely making a comeback, and I think this recipe is the ultimate. The wasabi paste can be found at an Asian market or specialty grocery store.

6 paper-thin slices of green onion,
   cut on the diagonal
2 ripe plum tomatoes, peeled, seeded,
   and cut into $1/4$-inch dice
$1^1/2$ teaspoons wasabi paste
6 fresh, shucked Olympia oysters
6 tablespoons Weinessiggut Doktorenhof's
   Gewürztraminer Eucalyptus Honey
   Vinegar (page 204)
6 tiny sprigs chervil

In each of 6 cold shot glasses, preferably the tall, straight-sided variety, layer the ingredients as follows: 1 slice of green onion, a small jumble of diced tomatoes, $1/4$ teaspoon wasabi paste, 1 Olympia oyster, 1 tablespoon of Gewürztraminer Eucalyptus Honey Vinegar, and 1 sprig of chervil. Serve immediately.

The Flavored Wine Vinegars of Germany

In Pfalz, in central Germany, the Wiedemann family converted their entire vineyard from wine to vinegar production and have been making unique, subtle wine and fruit-essence vinegars for more than ten years. With only a 3% to 5% acidity level, their vinegars are not as acidic as standard vinegars, which are at least 6%. In many of the vinegars the acidity is cut even more by the addition of some kind of honey, such as coffee blossom, orange blossom, eucalyptus, or chestnut honey, which also gives them their silky richness and subtle bite. Chefs most often use the vinegars as a refined flavoring in sauces or as a finishing touch for dishes. Now, however, in top German restaurants it has become popular to drink them as an aperitif to stimulate the appetite, or as a digestive to lighten the palate after a rich meal. Even Lufthansa airlines serves similar vinegars to first-class passengers.

Usually, vinegar is made from lesser quality wine. In fact, the word "vinegar" comes from the French *vin aigre*, meaning sour wine. In the wine business, vinegar is considered a by-product, a way to use up wines that didn't make the grade and to generate a little extra income at the same time. The difference between the specialty German vinegars and other flavored vinegars on the market is that they are made from top-quality grapes and wines such as Auslese, Beerenauslese, and Trockenbeerenauslese, and even the elusive Eiswein. Some of the best wines that Germany has to offer are turned into vinegars labeled Elderberry, Pinot Noir, Muscatel, Lavender, Nettle, Balm, and Sage, among many others. Using these vinegars as a seasoning gives a dish a unique flavor. Naturally, it is costly and time-consuming to produce these vinegars, and thus their prices are virtually astronomical by the time they reach U.S. shores. Luckily, there are plenty of other ways to add a little frisson of acidity to a dish. Wiedemann vinegars can be ordered directly from the company; see page 204 for ordering information.

SANDWICHES AND LIGHT COURSES

Smoked Trout on Olive Focaccia with
Green Apple, Celery Root, and Horseradish Salad

Yields: 6 servings

If you don't have focaccia or baguettes on hand, a light, fluffy country bread will do just as well. Just toast the slices until golden, brush with olive oil, and rub with the cut side of a garlic clove. The flavors here are classically German, but I've put them together in my own way.

Trout Salad

1 rib celery, cut into ⅛-inch dice

2 Granny Smith apples, peeled, cored, and cut into ⅛-inch dice

2 tablespoons prepared horseradish

½ cup mayonnaise

¾ pound smoked trout, bones removed and flesh shredded

2 teaspoons freshly squeezed lemon juice or to taste

½ teaspoon salt

Freshly ground white pepper to taste

Sandwiches

¼ cup extra virgin olive oil

Salt and freshly ground black pepper

12 x 6-inch rectangle of olive bread or Focaccia Bread (page 145) or 9 (6-inch) lengths of baguette

3 cups (about 3 ounces) loosely packed frisée leaves

⅓ cup Balsamic Vinaigrette (page 193)

Trout Salad. In a medium bowl, combine all the ingredients. Toss together until evenly mixed and add the salt and white pepper.

Sandwiches. Preheat a grill or broiler to high heat. In a small bowl, combine the olive oil with salt and pepper to taste. Cut the focaccia into nine 1½-inch-wide, 6-inch-long strips. Then, slice each strip in half horizontally to make 18 open-faced sandwich bases. (Alternatively, split the baguette pieces horizontally). Brush both sides of the focaccia with the seasoned oil. Grill the bread for 1 to 2 minutes on each side, or until they have light grill marks. Transfer the slices to a work surface and spoon a thick layer of trout salad down the length of each piece of toast.

Fan out 3 of the open-faced sandwiches in the center of each of 6 serving plates. In a medium bowl, quickly toss the frisée with the vinaigrette. Place a small mound of dressed frisée to the side of the sandwiches on each plate and serve.

Seared Tuna Sandwiches on Grilled English Muffin Bread with Wasabi Mayonnaise

Yield: 4 servings

Whatever you do, don't skimp on the Wasabi Mayonnaise! You'll want to use it on lots of other sandwiches, especially those with fish and seafood, so be sure to make extra. It keeps for up to 4 days in the refrigerator. The wasabi powder is available at Asian and gourmet markets.

Wasabi Mayonnaise

2 teaspoons Japanese wasabi powder

1 tablespoon water

3/4 cup mayonnaise

Sandwiches

8 slices English Muffin Bread (page 141), grilled until slightly charred on one side, or 4 English muffins, split and grilled

4 leaves red leaf lettuce

1/4 cup grated daikon radish

4 (4 x 4 x 1/4-inch-thick) slices of sushi-quality Ahi tuna

Salt and freshly ground black pepper

1 tablespoon vegetable oil

1 small plum tomato, thinly sliced

1 1/3 cups Röckenwagner's Coleslaw (page 41)

Mayonnaise. In a small mixing bowl, combine the wasabi powder and water and mix to form a smooth paste. Add the mayonnaise, whisk to mix thoroughly, cover, and refrigerate until needed.

Sandwiches. Place a slice of English Muffin Bread, grilled side down, in the center of each of 4 serving plates. Spread each slice with the mayonnaise and top with a lettuce leaf and some of the grated daikon.

Season the slices of tuna with salt and pepper. In a nonstick skillet, heat the vegetable oil over medium-high heat until very hot. Add the tuna and sear for 10 seconds, then turn over and sear for another 10 seconds. Immediately drape a slice of the tuna over the daikon on each sandwich and top with a few tomato slices. Close the sandwiches with another slice of bread, grilled side up.

Cut each sandwich in half on the diagonal and place two halves on each of 4 servings plates. Place a scoop of the coleslaw to the side of the sandwiches, and serve immediately.

Pretzel Burgers with Swiss Cheese and French Fries

Yield: 4 servings

The pretzel bun is the key to this recipe. The bun is not as soft as a regular hamburger bun—it's slightly doughy and is a delicious complement to a good hamburger patty. If you follow my instructions for making the buns carefully, you'll have a truly winning combination.

4 (³/₈-inch-thick) slices of red onion

Burgers
1¹/₂ pounds 22% fat ground beef
2 shallots, finely chopped
1 teaspoon finely chopped flat-leaf parsley
Pinch of ground cayenne pepper
Salt and freshly ground black pepper
4 (³/₈-inch-thick) slices beefsteak tomato
4 Pretzel Buns, split (page 142)
8 thin slices Swiss cheese
4 large handfuls French Fries (page 181)

Onions. Preheat a grill or broiler to high heat and grill the onion slices for about 1 minute, or until they have light grill marks on each side. Set the slices aside. (Leave the grill on.)

Burgers. In a mixing bowl, combine the ground beef with the shallots, parsley, cayenne, and salt and pepper. Form 4 loose patties. Grill the burgers for 4 to 6 minutes on each side for medium-rare, or to the desired doneness.

While the patties are cooking, grill the buns, cut sides down, for about 1 minute and then transfer to 4 warm serving plates. Top the burgers with the tomato, grilled onion, and cheese slices and continue to grill just until the cheese is melted.

Assembly. Place the burgers on the bottom halves of the pretzel buns and close with the top halves. Place the fries to the side of the burgers and serve immediately.

Grilled Marinated Portobello Mushroom Sandwich (front left); Zweiblewaie (front center); Pretzel Burger with Swiss Cheese and French Fries (back center)

Zweiblewaie (German/Alsatian Onion Tart)

Yield: 12 appetizer servings or 24 hors d'oeuvres

This is a traditional fall dish served on the border of Germany and Alsace. Every year during the wine-grape harvest, there is a week or so when people drink the new, unfiltered wine. The cloudy liquid is not really wine yet—it's fruit juice in which the sugars have not yet converted to alcohol. It usually takes about a week for the wine to "turn," depending on the temperature at which it's kept. Restaurants try to serve the wine when it is just at the point of turning so that people can actually experience the process of the fruit sugars converting into alcohol: tasters might try a glass from the barrel at 6 PM that is sweet and juicelike, and then have a glass from the same barrel at 9 the same night and find it has suddenly become quite potent. Traditional foods for this wine-tasting are freshly harvested walnuts and this slightly addictive tart. Add a salad and glass of fruity wine, and the tart makes a superb dinner for six. (See photo on page 79.)

Pastry
3 cups all-purpose flour
¹/₂ ounce fresh yeast or ¹/₄ ounce active dry yeast
¹/₂ teaspoon sugar
³/₄ cup lukewarm water
¹/₄ cup olive oil
Pinch of salt

Filling
2 tablespoons olive oil
10 white onions, peeled, cut in half lengthwise, and thinly sliced
Scant 1 tablespoon cumin seeds
¹/₄ teaspoon salt
Freshly ground black pepper to taste
4 large eggs, lightly beaten
1³/₄ cups half-and-half
2 teaspoons sweet paprika
Salt
Freshly ground white pepper
¹/₂ pound lean bacon, cut into ¹/₄-inch dice (see Note)

Pastry. Place the flour in a large, warmed bowl and make a well in the center. In a glass measuring cup, combine the yeast, sugar, and ¹/₂ cup of the warm water, and stir to dissolve slightly. Set aside to proof, about 10 minutes. Stir in the remaining ¹/₄ cup warm water and the olive oil.

Pour the yeast mixture into the well in the center of the flour and begin drawing the flour into the center, blending until all the liquid is absorbed, adding the salt toward the end. Turn the dough out onto a lightly floured work surface and knead until it is smooth and elastic. Lightly oil a large bowl and place the dough in it. Turn the dough to coat it with oil, cover with plastic wrap, and set it aside to rise in a very warm, moist place. When the dough has doubled in size and appears spongy and dimpled, punch it down, cover with a kitchen towel, and start making the filling.

Filling. Heat a large, heavy skillet over medium-low heat and add the olive oil. Add the onions and sauté, covered, for 7 to 8 minutes, or until translucent. Stir in the cumin seeds, salt, and black pepper. Set aside to cool.

Assembly. Preheat the oven to 375°. Gently turn the dough out onto a large floured surface and roll it into a 20 x 15-inch rectangle. Press the dough firmly into the bottom and sides of a lightly oiled 18 x 13-inch baking sheet with 1-inch-high sides.

In a large bowl, beat together the eggs, half-and-half, paprika, salt, and white pepper. Distribute the onions evenly over the base of the crust. Gently pour in the custard mixture, taking care not to disturb the even distribution of the onions. Scatter the bacon evenly over the top and bake in the hot oven for 30 minutes, or until the custard is set in the center and the bacon is crisp. Cool for at least 10 minutes, then slice into rectangles to serve as an appetizer or into small squares to serve as an hors d'oeuvre.

The tart should be served warm. If it has cooled, reheat in a 325° oven for 15 to 20 minutes.

Note: It is traditional to let the bacon cook on top of the tart, but if you want to cook out a bit of the fat, fry it over low heat for a few minutes until it is slightly golden but not crisp, drain on paper towels, and proceed as directed.

Working with Yeast

I usually call for fresh yeast in my recipes because that's what we use in the kitchen and I find it easier to work with than the dry variety. It seems somehow more alive and, after all, a yeast dough is a living thing. Any bakery will be happy to sell you a lump of fresh yeast (usually much more than you need) for a few pennies, or you can purchase 0.6-ounce cakes of fresh yeast at the supermarket. Here's how the various forms differ from one another:

Fresh yeast does not show much activity when mixed with water, and the temperature of the water is not particularly important. The yeast begins its work only when mixed with food (sugar or flour) and left at a warm temperature. It easily survives freezing; in fact it is more active at -10° than at 40°. This means not only can you freeze individual cakes of fresh yeast, you can also freeze a yeast dough at any stage before it is baked and it won't lose any of its rising power.

Dry yeast is extremely sensitive to water temperature. It must be reconstituted in water that is between 105° and 110°. Any lower or higher temperature will result in almost complete loss of fermenting power. Given the correct temperature of water, dry yeast can sometimes be very active even before it is fed (sugar is added), expending much of its energy before it comes into contact with the dough. This is why it is important you don't leave the yeast proofing for too long—once you see a nice thick frothy head, it's time to mix the dough. If the yeast does not become frothy, it is dead and you must start again with new yeast. If you use dry yeast for the recipes in this book, simply use half the amount (or use the conversions below) and be sure to measure the temperature of the water accurately.

$1/2$ ounce fresh yeast = 1 (0.6-ounce) cake of compressed yeast = 1 ($1/4$-ounce) envelope dry yeast = $2 1/4$ teaspoons bulk dry yeast

Smoked Turkey Sandwiches with
Blue Cheese, Watercress, and Cranberry Chutney

Yield: 4 servings

This combination features some of the best Thanksgiving flavors, and is wonderful year-round. If you don't like blue cheese, by all means leave it out, but don't omit the cranberry chutney or you'll take away the sandwich's character. This is quite a tall sandwich and definitely needs to be skewered to make it to the table intact. (See photo on page 84.)

4 (3½ x 3½-inch) rectangles Focaccia Bread (page 145)

1 cup Cranberry-Apple Chutney (page 196)

12 slices high-quality smoked turkey breast (about 6 ounces)

3 tomatoes, sliced ¼ inch thick

½ pound domestic blue cheese

3 cups (about 3 ounces) loosely packed watercress leaves and tender stems, washed and dried

Sandwiches. Split the focaccia rectangles horizontally. Lay the bottom 4 slices on the work surface and spread each with an equal amount of the chutney. Fold the turkey slices loosely in half and overlap three of them on top of the chutney. Top the turkey with some of the tomato slices, then crumble about 2 tablespoons of blue cheese on each sandwich. Top each one with about ¾ cup of the watercress leaves and close with the remaining slices of focaccia, pressing down gently.

Assembly. Slice the sandwiches in half on the diagonal, skewer each half with a decorative toothpick, and serve immediately.

Grilled Marinated Portobello Mushroom Sandwiches

Yield: 4 servings

This is a very juicy, very substantial, somewhat drippy sandwich. The portobello is a meaty mushroom, and when prepared this way, it has so much flavor it's almost like a steak. (See photo on page 79.)

Sundried Tomato Spread
1 cup dry-packed sundried tomatoes
1 small clove garlic
2 tablespoons extra virgin olive oil

4 large Marinated Portobello Mushrooms (page 197)
4 (^{1}/$_2$-inch-thick) slices red onion
8 (^{1}/$_2$-inch-thick) slices country-style olive bread or other rustic bread
1^1/$_2$ cups (about 1^1/$_2$ ounces) loosely packed baby arugula leaves
2 roasted red bell peppers, stemmed, seeded, peeled, and torn into 1-inch pieces (page 202)
4 thin slices Swiss cheese

Spread. Place the sundried tomatoes in a small saucepan and add water to cover. Bring the water to a simmer, then remove from the heat, place a small bowl or saucer in the pan to keep the tomatoes submerged, and let stand for 20 minutes. When supple and cool enough to handle, squeeze the tomatoes dry and place in a blender or food processor. Add the garlic and olive oil and process until smooth, scraping down the sides of the bowl as necessary. Transfer the spread to a small bowl, cover and set aside. (The spread will keep, covered, in the refrigerator for up to 10 days.)

Sandwiches. Preheat the oven to 325° and preheat a grill or broiler to high heat. Place the mushrooms on a rack set over a dry roasting pan and dry in the hot oven for 5 minutes. Transfer the mushrooms to the grill and grill for 2 minutes on each side, or until they have light grill marks and are slightly tender. At the same time, grill the onion slices on both sides and the bread slices on one side until they also have light grill marks. Cut the portobellos at a sharp angle into ^{1}/$_2$-inch slices.

Assembly. Lay 4 slices of bread grill-mark side down on the work surface and preheat the broiler to medium-high. Spread each slice of bread with about 1 tablespoon of the Sundried Tomato Spread. Scatter a generous layer of baby arugula leaves over the bread and top with a slice of grilled onion, a few pieces of roasted red pepper, and 1 of the sliced portobellos. Top with a slice of cheese and place under the broiler just long enough to melt the cheese. Quickly close each sandwich with the remaining slices of bread and serve immediately.

Pear and Brie Sandwiches on Walnut Bread

Yield: 4 servings

The combination of pear and brie is fairly common, but it's not so common to find them together on a sandwich. Make sure you get the really sweet, juicy butter pears and don't skimp with them; the pear flavor must be prominent to stand up to the richness of the slightly melted brie. If the pears are sweet and ripe, there is no need to peel them. My Walnut Bread is ideal for this sandwich, but if you buy the bread use a substantial sourdough or rye walnut bread.

Tarragon Mayonnaise
2 tablespoons mayonnaise
2 teaspoons minced fresh tarragon

Sandwiches
8 (¹/₂-inch-thick) slices Walnut Sourdough (page 140) or other sourdough bread
3 sweet, ripe pears (such as Williams or other butter pears), peeled (if desired), cored, and thinly sliced
2 cups (about 2 ounces) loosely packed watercress leaves and tender stems, washed and dried
4 ounces (about ²/₃ cup) Pickled Onions (page 198), cut into julienne
³/₄ pound ripe brie, sliced ¹/₄ inch thick with rind on
2 teaspoons Dijon-style mustard

Mayonnaise. In a small bowl, whisk together the mayonnaise and tarragon and set aside.

Sandwiches. Preheat the broiler to medium-high heat. Toast the bread until golden brown and place 4 of the slices toasted side down on the work surface. Spread about ¹/₂ tablespoon of the mayonnaise on each of the bottom slices of bread and add one-quarter of the sliced pears. Top with a generous layer of watercress leaves and about one-quarter of the pickled onions, arranging all of the ingredients evenly over the bread. Arrange slices of brie over the pickled onions and place the sandwiches under the hot broiler. Grill only until the brie begins to melt, but is not bubbly or golden.

Assembly. Spread each of the top slices of bread with ¹/₂ teaspoon of the mustard. Place each sandwich on a plate, close with the remaining slices of bread, and serve immediately.

Pear and Brie Sandwiches on Walnut Bread (left) and Smoked Trout on Olive Focaccia with Green Apple, Celery Root, and Horseradish Salad

Potato, Corn, and Red Pepper Risotto

Yield: 6 servings

In this risotto I have replaced the traditional arborio rice with starchy potatoes. The potatoes should be carefully diced to a size just larger than a grain of rice, and you must be careful not to overcook them or they will lose their shape. This is a master recipe that can be the basis for many variations once you have learned to cook the potatoes to the right doneness. I like this version better than all the other potato risottos I've made because it has everything going for it—creaminess, a satisfying texture, and a lovely, bright color. The dish must be served immediately; it doesn't wait well.

1 pound russet potatoes, peeled and cut into
   $1/4$-inch dice (about 3 cups)

$1^1/_2$ cups fresh corn kernels (about 3 ears)

$2^3/_4$ cups Red Bell Pepper Juice (page 203)

$1^1/_2$ teaspoons Hungarian paprika

$1/4$ teaspoon ground cayenne pepper

1 to 3 teaspoons freshly squeezed lemon juice

3 tablespoons heavy cream

6 tablespoons unsalted butter, cut into 6 pieces

$1/2$ cup freshly grated Parmesan cheese

$3/4$ teaspoon salt

$1/4$ teaspoon freshly ground white pepper

Sprigs of fresh chervil, for garnish

12 scallions, trimmed and grilled until lightly
   charred, for garnish

Risotto. In a large nonreactive saucepan combine the potato cubes, corn kernels, pepper juice, paprika, and cayenne. Bring to a simmer and cook, stirring frequently, for 8 to 10 minutes, or until the potatoes are just tender and the juice is reduced by about one-third. Add 1 teaspoon of the lemon juice, taste, and add more if needed. Continue to reduce and, when the mixture is almost dry, add the cream and decrease the heat to low. Cook for 1 minute more, then add the butter, stirring until it is absorbed. Remove from the heat and stir in the Parmesan, salt, and white pepper.

Assembly. Spoon the risotto into warmed bowls, garnish each with a few sprigs of chervil and 2 grilled scallions, and serve immediately.

Carrot Risotto

Yield: 6 servings

This is a fun and interesting vegetarian dish. If you want to make a special vegetarian dinner, serve this risotto with an assortment of grilled vegetables (especially the large portobello mushrooms). Start the meal with a light salad and finish with a refreshing dessert, like a berry or fruit dish, as the risotto is fairly substantial.

5 cups homemade carrot juice

2 cups Red Bell Pepper Juice (page 203)

1/4 cup plus 1 tablespoon unsalted butter

2 large shallots, finely chopped

1 small clove garlic, finely chopped

2 1/4 cups arborio rice, rinsed

3/4 teaspoon salt

1/2 teaspoon freshly ground white pepper

1/4 cup heavy cream

1/4 cup grated Grana Padano or imported
  Parmigiano-Reggiano cheese

Risotto. In a medium saucepan, combine the carrot and red pepper juices over medium heat. Heat to just below boiling, then lower the temperature and keep the mixture hot but not simmering.

In a large, heavy saucepan, heat 2 tablespoons of the butter over medium-low heat. Add the shallots and garlic and sauté, stirring occasionally, for 6 to 7 minutes, or until softened but not brown. Stir in the rice and cook until it is very hot and well coated with the butter, but not toasted or browned. Increase the heat to medium-high and begin adding the hot juice mixture, one ladleful at a time, stirring until the liquid is absorbed before adding more. (All the liquid should be added and absorbed in about 20 minutes.) Add the salt, white pepper, and cream and taste for seasoning.

Remove the pan from the heat and immediately stir in the cheese and the remaining 3 tablespoons butter until evenly blended. Serve immediately.

Meze Plate

Yield: 12 to 15 servings

The United States, particularly California, has seen a Mediterranean food craze in recent years and I think there are several reasons for this besides the fact that it's a healthful cuisine. One explanation is that the climate in Southern California is very similar to that of the Mediterranean, and it lends itself to these sunny flavors. For those who don't live in a Mediterranean climate and wish they did— I know I certainly did when I lived in Germany and Chicago—Mediterranean cuisine is the perfect escape. This dish was very popular at our former sister restaurant in Santa Monica, Fama.

These recipes make enough for a crowd: the Melitzana recipe makes about 1 quart, the Hummus recipe yields about 3¹/₄ cups, and the Tzatziki recipe makes about 2 cups. If you're not cooking for a group, the extra dip keeps well in the refrigerator for a few days. All of these recipes require advance preparation, so be sure to start the night before you plan to serve them.

Melitzana

4 medium eggplants, halved lengthwise

2 cloves garlic, coarsely chopped

¹/₄ cup extra virgin olive oil

2 tablespoons plain yogurt

¹/₂ teaspoon salt

Freshly ground black pepper to taste

1 teaspoon distilled white vinegar

1 tablespoon finely chopped fresh dill

2 shallots, finely chopped

Hummus

³/₄ pound dried garbanzo beans, soaked overnight in cold water to cover, or 3 cups cooked or canned drained beans, juice reserved

1 teaspoon salt

³/₄ cup tahini paste

1 teaspoon finely chopped garlic

³/₄ cup freshly squeezed lemon juice

Salt and freshly ground black pepper to taste

³/₄ cup extra virgin olive oil

Tzatziki

1¹/₂ cups plain yogurt

¹/₂ European cucumber, peeled, seeded, and coarsely grated

1 teaspoon salt

1 small clove garlic, finely chopped

Freshly ground white pepper to taste

¹/₃ cup extra virgin olive oil

2 tablespoons freshly squeezed lemon juice

1 teaspoon finely chopped fresh dill, or ¹/₂ teaspoon dried

24 rounds pita bread, cut into wedges and grilled

Melitzana. Preheat the oven to 400°. Using a large fork and tongs, char the eggplants over a gas flame until they are blistered and black all over. (You may want to do this over 2 burners at once to save time.) Transfer the eggplants to a large roasting pan and finish cooking them in the oven for 30 minutes, or until the flesh is very tender. Remove the eggplants from the oven and let cool. Line a sieve with a layer of cheesecloth and set it over a bowl. When cool enough to handle, peel the eggplants, and discard the charred skin. (Don't worry if a few pieces remain.) Transfer the eggplant flesh to the lined sieve, cover, and refrigerate overnight while it drains.

The next day, bring the 4 corners of the cheese-cloth together and gently squeeze even more of the excess moisture out of eggplant. In the bowl of a food processor, combine the eggplant flesh with the garlic cloves and purée until very smooth, scraping down the sides of the bowl as necessary. With the motor running, add the olive oil in a thin, steady stream, then add the yogurt and process until the mixture is a smooth paste. Stir in the salt, pepper, vinegar, dill, and shallots. Store covered in the refrigerator until ready to serve. (The Melitzana can be prepared up to 2 days in advance.)

Hummus. If using uncooked garbanzos, drain the beans. Place them in a large saucepan with fresh water to cover by about 2 inches. Bring the water to a simmer over medium-high heat and cook the beans for 30 minutes, partially covered. Stir in the salt and cook for $1^1/_2$ to 2 hours more, or until they are very soft.

Drain the beans, reserving $^1/_2$ cup of the cooking water, and put them through a ricer or food mill into the large bowl of a heavy-duty electric mixer. Add the tahini, garlic, lemon juice, and salt and pepper. Beat all the ingredients well, adding the olive oil in a thin, steady stream as the mixer runs. Whenever the mixture gets too clumpy to move easily, add 1 or 2 tablespoons of the cook-ing water to thin it (you shouldn't need more than $^1/_4$ cup). Store covered in the refrigerator until ready to serve. (The hummus can be pre-pared up to 3 days in advance.)

Tzatziki. Line a fine sieve with a double thickness of cheesecloth and set it over a bowl. Place the yogurt in the sieve, cover with plastic wrap, and drain for 8 hours or overnight in the refrigerator.

The next day, place the cucumber in a large colander and set over a plate. Add the salt, toss, and let drain for 45 minutes. Wrap the cucum-ber in a kitchen towel and squeeze out as much of the remaining moisture as possible.

In the large bowl of a heavy-duty electric mixer, combine the yogurt, garlic, and white pepper and beat on slow speed. Add the olive oil in a thin, steady stream as the mixer runs. Stir in the cucumber and lemon juice, then taste and adjust the seasonings as necessary. Store, covered, in the refrigerator until ready to serve, and add the dill just before serving. (The Tzatziki can be prepared, without adding the dill, up to 3 days in advance.)

Assembly. Place the Melitzana, Hummus, and Tzatsiki in medium serving bowls. Wrap the pita wedges in a cloth napkin and place in a basket. Serve immediately.

Orrechiette with Rapini, Garlic, and Cherry Tomatoes

Yield: 6 servings

I often compare rapini to arugula. They may be very different in appearance, but rapini has the same tartness that can lift a dish to a whole new level. It is also referred to as Italian broccoli, and is certainly what gives this rustic and homey pasta dish its character.

It might seem as if the garlic would completely over- power this dish, but blanching it removes its sharp flavor, leaving only the creamy sweetness we all love.

Sauce

1 pound rapini

10 large cloves garlic

1 tablespoon extra virgin olive oil

1½ teaspoons crushed red pepper flakes

1½ cups Chicken Stock (page 186)

¾ teaspoon salt

Freshly ground black pepper to taste

Pasta

1 pound dried imported orrechiette pasta

1 tablespoon salt

6 tablespoons unsalted butter, cut into 6 pieces

30 cherry tomatoes, halved

¾ cup grated fresh Parmesan cheese

Sauce. If the rapini stems are thicker than ³/8 inch, peel them. Cut the stems into 2-inch lengths, discard the large, tough leaves, and separate the tender leaves and florets into 2-inch pieces. Bring a stockpot of water to a boil. Add the rapini and blanch for 2 minutes, or until al dente. Shock in ice water, drain well, and set aside.

Place the garlic in a small saucepan and add cold water to cover by 2 inches. Bring to a boil. Blanch for 1 minute, then drain in a colander. Refill the saucepan with cold water, add the garlic again, and bring to a boil. Again, blanch for 1 minute, then drain and slice paper thin.

Heat a very large skillet over medium heat and add the olive oil. Sauté the garlic, stirring frequently, until golden, about 3 minutes. Add the pepper flakes and rapini and sauté for another 3 minutes. Add the stock, salt, and pepper, and bring to a simmer. Reduce, stirring occasionally, until only about ½ cup of liquid remains and the rapini is very tender.

Pasta. While the sauce is cooking, bring a stock- pot of water to a boil and add the salt. Cook the orrechiette until al dente, then drain well.

Assembly. Add the pasta to the skillet with the sauce. Toss together until the pasta is evenly coated, then add the butter and stir until it is absorbed. Add the cherry tomatoes and toss until evenly distributed. Remove from the heat and stir in the Parmesan. Taste, adjust the seasonings as necessary, and serve immediately in large heated bowls.

Goat Cheese–Topped Pork Tenderloins Rolled in Cracked Pepper with Spätzle

Yield: 6 servings

This dish is one of my all-time favorites, partly because it features the type of contrasts I always strive for in my food. It has soft and crisp textures and sweet and sour flavors that almost explode in your mouth.

3 (12-ounce) pork tenderloins, trimmed of
   fat and sinew
1/2 cup coarsely cracked black pepper
Salt
8-ounce log Montrachet goat cheese
2 tablespoons olive oil

Bell Peppers
2 tablespoons olive oil
2 roasted yellow bell peppers, stemmed, seeded,
   peeled, and cut into 1/2-inch strips (page 202)
2 roasted red bell peppers, stemmed, seeded,
   peeled, and cut into 1/2-inch strips (page 202)

36 large fresh basil leaves
1 recipe Spätzle (page 180), hot
1 1/2 cups Veal Demiglace (page 188), warm

Tenderloins. Slice each tenderloin into 6 equal pieces and pound them gently to flatten into medallions about 2 inches in diameter and 1/2 to 3/4 inch thick. Spread the cracked pepper evenly on a tray. Gently roll only the edges of the medallions in the pepper to coat them evenly. Do not press while rolling or too much pepper will adhere to the medallions. Season with salt and set aside. Using a wire cheese slicer, or fishing line or quilting thread held taut, cut the goat cheese into 18 equal slices, and set aside.

Preheat the oven to 375°. Heat two ovenproof, nonstick skillets over medium-high heat and add 1 tablespoon of the olive oil to each pan. Add the medallions and sear for 2 minutes on each side, or until slightly firm and browned. Transfer the pans to the oven for 5 minutes more for pork that is still slightly pink or 10 minutes more for well done. Two minutes before the pork will be done to your liking, place a disc of goat cheese atop each medallion and let it soften and slightly melt.

Bell Peppers. While the pork finishes cooking, heat a large, heavy skillet over medium-high heat and add the olive oil. Add the peppers and sauté, stirring occasionally, for about 3 minutes.

Assembly. Mound an equal portion of the spätzle in the center of each of 6 heated serving plates. Place 3 pork medallions around the spätzle and set a pair of basil leaves between the medallions. Top the basil leaves with a jumble of bell peppers. Drizzle the edge of the plates with the demiglace and serve immediately.

Sautéed Louisiana Gulf Shrimp on Basil Fettucine with Lobster Sauce

Yield: 6 servings

This is a dish I used to make eleven years ago when I opened the first Röckenwagner, and it has stood the test of time—I'd be afraid to take it off the menu now. It is worth taking the time and effort to make this lobster sauce, which I use in several other dishes, such as the crab soufflé (page 58). When combined with the pan juices from the shrimp, the flavors become exceedingly refined and complex. If you prefer, you may substitute 1½ pounds imported dried fettucine for the homemade noodles.

Basil Fettucine

5 cups (about 5 ounces) loosely packed
   spinach leaves

½ cup firmly packed basil leaves

1 tablespoon extra virgin olive oil

2 tablespoons water

2 large eggs

1 large egg yolk

3 cups all-purpose flour

Rice flour for dusting

Lobster Sauce

2 tablespoons vegetable oil

4 shallots, finely chopped

1 clove garlic, finely chopped

1 anchovy fillet, minced

1 teaspoon tomato paste

2 cups Lobster Stock (page 188)

⅓ cup heavy cream

1 teaspoon salt

Freshly ground black pepper to taste

Dash of Tabasco sauce

½ teaspoon freshly squeezed lemon juice

1 cup cold unsalted butter, cut into ½-inch cubes

2 tablespoons extra virgin olive oil

36 medium Louisiana Gulf shrimp
   (about 2 pounds)

Salt and freshly ground black pepper to taste

9 plum tomatoes, peeled, seeded, and diced

Deep-fried basil leaves (page 202), optional

Fettucine. Bring a pan of water to a simmer. Add the spinach leaves and blanch for 15 seconds. Remove with a skimmer, then shock in ice water. Spread the leaves out on paper towels to drain. Squeeze any remaining water out of the leaves, then chop finely.

In a food processor, combine the basil, olive oil, water, and spinach and process for 2 to 3 minutes, scraping down the sides of the bowl as necessary, until the mixture becomes a very fine purée. With the motor running, add the eggs and egg yolks. Add the flour and process until the dough forms a rough ball (this shouldn't take more than 15 seconds). If the dough does not form a ball, you will need to add 1 to 2 tablespoons of water and process until it does. Turn the dough out onto a lightly floured surface and knead until it is smooth and stiff. Cover with a kitchen towel and let rest for 1 to 2 hours. Using a manual pasta machine (do not use an electric pasta extruder), roll the dough out into thin sheets and cut into fettucine-width noodles. Sprinkle rice flour over the noodles and toss gently to keep them from sticking to each other. Set aside on a plate lightly dusted with rice flour until ready to cook. (The uncooked noodles can be refrigerated, loosely covered, for up to 2 hours.)

Sauce. Heat a large saucepan over medium heat and add the vegetable oil. Add the shallots and sauté for 2 to 3 minutes, or until softened. Add the garlic, anchovy, and tomato paste and sauté for 1 minute more. Stir in the stock and bring the liquid to a rapid simmer. Reduce the liquid to one-quarter of its original volume, so that about $1/2$ cup of liquid remains. Add the cream and reduce again to just less than $1/2$ cup of syrupy liquid. Stir in the salt, pepper, Tabasco, and lemon juice. Decrease the heat to very low and whisk in the butter a few pieces at a time, continuing to whisk just until the sauce is emulsified. (Do not let the sauce boil.) Just before the last piece of butter has been absorbed, remove from the heat and whisk until the sauce is smooth. Strain through a fine sieve into a clean pan and set aside (no longer than 20 minutes).

Assembly. Bring a large saucepan of water to a boil and add the salt. (If you are using dried pasta, begin cooking it now, before cooking the shrimp, as it will take longer to cook than the fresh pasta.) At the same time, heat a large skillet over high heat until it is very hot, then add the olive oil. Add the shrimp and sauté in the hot oil for about 2 minutes, tossing them once or twice while they cook and seasoning with salt and pepper. Remove the pan from the heat, add the Lobster Sauce and tomatoes and toss well. Cover and keep warm.

Bring a stockpot of water to a boil. Add the basil fettucine and cook for about $1^{1}/_{2}$ minutes, or until al dente. Using kitchen tongs, make a nest of fettucine on each of 6 heated dinner plates. Spoon the warm sauce into the center of the pasta nests and garnish with a few sprigs of fried basil.

Glazed Shrimp on Crisp Chow Mein with Fermented Black Bean Sauce

Yield: 4 servings

This is one of my favorite dishes, hands-down. It was inspired by many visits to authentic Chinese restaurants with my good friend Gordon Lee, who likes to take me to the brightly lit eating halls of downtown Los Angeles or Monterey Park, where I am often the only non-Chinese customer. He makes me try things I never dreamed I would eat, and then watches my reaction, grinning all the time. I thank him for keeping me on my toes and adding a wonderful new dimension to my cooking. The mirin wine and fermented black beans can be found at Asian markets.

Chow Mein Cakes

½ teaspoon salt

1 pound fresh Chinese chow mein noodles

3 to 4 tablespoons peanut oil

Black Bean Sauce

¼ cup dried fermented black beans

½ cup plum wine

2 tablespoons vegetable oil

½ small yellow onion, finely chopped

3 scallions, white and light green parts only, finely chopped

¼ cup coarsely chopped fresh cilantro

1 teaspoon finely chopped garlic

1 teaspoon finely chopped shallot

1 teaspoon grated fresh ginger

2 cups mirin wine

1 cup Veal Stock (page 189)

1 cup cold unsalted butter, cut into ½-inch cubes

½ teaspoon salt

Freshly ground black pepper to taste

1 teaspoon freshly squeezed lime juice

Snow Pea Salad

1 cup snow peas, trimmed

2 ripe red plums, pitted, quartered, and cut into ¼-inch dice

¼ cup Sesame Vinaigrette (page 65)

1½ tablespoons vegetable oil

12 to 16 large shrimp, with tails on (about 10 ounces)

2 tablespoons Shrimp Glaze (page 191)

1 tablespoon dark sesame oil

12 (4-inch) lengths fresh chives

Noodle Cakes. Bring a large saucepan of water to a boil and add the salt. Add the noodles and cook just until soft, about 3 minutes, then drain well and dry briefly on paper towels.

In a 6-inch skillet, heat 2 teaspoons of the peanut oil over high heat. When very hot, place one-quarter of the cooked noodles in the pan, spreading them out evenly and pressing gently to compact them into a rough pancake. Cook for 3 minutes, invert onto a plate, add 1 to 2 more teaspoons of peanut oil to the pan if it is dry, and then transfer the noodle pancake back to the pan to cook the other side. Cook for 5 minutes more, then drain on paper towels. Repeat three more times until you have 4 crispy noodle cakes. Set aside, uncovered, for up to 1 hour while you finish the dish.

Sauce. In a small saucepan, combine the black beans and plum wine. Reduce the mixture to half of its original volume over medium-high heat. Set aside.

continued

Glazed Shrimp *continued*

Heat the vegetable oil in a large skillet or sauce-pan over medium-high heat. Add the onion, scallions, and cilantro and sauté for 2 to 3 minutes, or until they begin to soften. Add the garlic, shallot, and ginger, and continue to sauté until golden brown, about 3 minutes. Stir in the mirin and stock and bring to a rapid simmer. Reduce the liquid to one-third of its original volume, so that about 1 cup remains, then strain the sauce through a fine sieve into a clean pan, pressing firmly on the solids to extract any remaining liquid. Discard the solids. Stir the black bean and plum wine mixture into the strained liquid, and, over very low heat, begin whisking in the cubes of butter. Wait until each one is absorbed and the sauce is emulsified before adding more. (Do not allow the mixture to boil.) When the last cube of butter is almost absorbed, remove from the heat and continue to whisk until the sauce is smooth. Stir in the salt, pepper, and lime juice. Set aside, covered, while you finish the dish (no longer than 20 minutes).

Salad. Bring a pan of water to a boil. Add the snow peas and blanch for 1 minute. Remove with a skimmer, shock in ice water, then drain and slice thinly lengthwise. In a small bowl, combine the snow peas, diced plums, and vinaigrette and set aside.

Assembly. In a low oven, warm the noodle cakes on 4 serving plates. Heat a large skillet over high heat and add the vegetable oil. Add the shrimp and sauté for about 1 minute on each side. Reduce the heat to very low, add the shrimp glaze, and stir to coat the shrimp evenly. Cover the pan and cook for 3 minutes more, then remove from the heat.

Remove the noodle cakes from the oven, divide the glazed shrimp among the plates, placing them on the noodles. Spoon some of the black bean sauce around the shrimp. Place a small mound of salad in the center of the shrimp and drizzle a few drops of the sesame oil around the edges of the plates. Garnish with the chives and serve immediately.

Crispy Striped Bass on a Ragout of Sunchokes, Pearl Onions, and Asparagus with Spicy Plum Wine Sauce

Yield: 6 servings

Lately, I have been using the technique I use to cook the bass in this recipe with other types of fish such as salmon, snapper, and whitefish. I sear the fish skin side down for nearly all of its cooking time and then quickly finish it on its other side. The crispness of the seared skin balances the creamy texture of the flesh. Urge your fishmonger or market to offer more cuts of fish with the skin left on!

Spicy Plum Wine Sauce

1 750-ml. bottle plum wine
1 tablespoon coriander seeds
1 small piece star anise
1 teaspoon crushed red pepper flakes
2 teaspoons grated fresh ginger
1 clove garlic, thinly sliced
1 large shallot, thinly sliced
3^1/$_2$ cups Veal Stock (page 189)
1 cup Chicken Stock (page 186)

Ragout

^{3}/$_4$ pound sunchokes, peeled and cut into
   ^{3}/$_4$-inch chunks, or 6 to 8 baby artichoke
   bottoms, trimmed
^{3}/$_4$ pound pearl onions, peeled
^{3}/$_4$ pound asparagus, stems peeled and cut
   into 1^1/$_2$-inch lengths on the diagonal
2 tablespoons clarified butter (page 202)
^{1}/$_2$ teaspoon salt
Freshly ground black pepper to taste

Fish

6 (5-ounce) fillets of striped bass, pin
   bones removed, with skin on
Salt and freshly ground black pepper
1 tablespoon vegetable oil

Sauce. In a large saucepan, combine the plum wine with the coriander seeds, star anise, pepper flakes, ginger, garlic, and shallot and bring to a simmer over medium-high heat. Simmer until reduced to about one-quarter of its original volume, about 1 cup, and slightly syrupy. Add the veal and chicken stocks and reduce to about 1^1/$_3$ cups, until an intensely flavored, syrupy liquid remains. Strain and set aside.

Ragout. Bring a large saucepan full of water to a boil. Add the sunchokes and blanch for 5 minutes, or until al dente, shock in ice water, and then drain on paper towels. Repeat with the pearl onions, also blanching them for about 5 minutes and setting aside on paper towels to drain. Finally, blanch the asparagus for 6 minutes, shock in ice water, and then drain. Heat a large skillet over medium-high heat and add the clarified butter. Add all three vegetables and sauté, tossing every minute or so, until they are tender, about 4 minutes. Add the salt and pepper and set aside while you cook the fish.

Fish. Season both sides of the bass with salt and pepper. Heat a large cast iron pan over medium-low heat. When the pan is hot, add the vegetable oil. Cook the fish, skin side down, very slowly, so that the skin becomes crispy. (You may want to cook the fish in 2 pans at once.) While you are cooking the fish, gently reheat the sauce. When the fish is almost done, about 5 minutes, turn it over and cook for about 30 seconds more, then remove from the heat.

Assembly. Make a bed of vegetable ragout in each of 6 large heated serving bowls. Place a bass fillet skin side up on the vegetables and divide the sauce among the bowls, pouring it around the edges. Serve immediately.

Grilled Sea Bass with Orange and Red Onion Sauce and Citrus Couscous

Yield: 6 servings

This is a very simple dish that has great flavors and is also low in fat. It is one from a series of lowfat recipes featuring fruit and vegetable juices that I developed for Food & Wine. *The red onion sauce and citrus couscous are great additions to anyone's repertoire, and the whole dish makes a delightful summer repast.*

Sauce

1½ tablespoons olive oil

1 pound red onions, peeled and cut lengthwise into ¼-inch slices

2 cups freshly squeezed orange juice

2 tablespoons finely chopped flat-leaf parsley

Dash of Tabasco sauce

Pinch of ground coriander

¼ teaspoon salt

Freshly ground black pepper to taste

Couscous

3 cups light Chicken Stock (page 186) or vegetable stock

Grated zest of 1 orange

Grated zest of 1 lemon

Grated zest of 1 lime

¼ teaspoon Chinese chile paste

2 tablespoons extra virgin olive oil

1½ cups instant couscous

½ teaspoon salt

¼ teaspoon freshly ground black pepper

Fish

6 (4- to 5-ounce) skinless, boneless sea bass fillets, about 1 inch thick

1 tablespoon olive oil

Salt and freshly ground black pepper

½ lemon

Sprigs of fresh chervil, for garnish

Sauce. In a large nonreactive skillet heat the olive oil over medium-low heat. Add the red onions and sauté, stirring occasionally, for about 10 minutes, or until softened but not browned. Add the orange juice and bring the mixture to a boil. Simmer until the liquid is reduced by half, about 10 minutes. Remove from the heat and stir in the parsley, Tabasco, coriander, salt, and pepper. Set aside.

Couscous. In a medium saucepan, combine the stock, citrus zests, chile paste, and olive oil. Over medium heat, bring the mixture just to a boil, then immediately stir in the couscous. Remove from the heat, cover the pan, and let stand until tender, about 10 minutes. When all of the liquid has been absorbed, fluff the couscous with a fork and add the salt and pepper.

Fish. Brush the sea bass on all sides with the olive oil. Preheat a grill or broiler to medium-high. Season the fillets with salt and pepper and grill them for about 3 minutes on each side, or until done through and opaque. During the last minute of cooking, squeeze a little lemon juice over each fillet.

Assembly. Place a mound of couscous on each of 6 heated dinner plates and place a grilled fillet on top. Drizzle the sauce around the edges of the plates and garnish with a few sprigs of the chervil.

Pepper-Crusted Tuna on Braised Turnips with Olives and Leeks

Yield: 6 servings

Most of our customers who order this dish for the tuna end up loving the turnips. The combination of the turnips and the black olive sauce is a true winner. If you don't feel like making the olive crisps, you can use blue corn tortilla chips (preferably diamond shaped).

Olive Crisps
1/2 cup pitted kalamata olives
1 small clove garlic
2 tablespoons extra virgin olive oil
1 large egg yolk
1 large egg
3/4 cup fine cornmeal
2 to 3 tablespoons all-purpose flour
Vegetable oil for deep-frying

Olive Sauce
1 3/4 cups pitted kalamata olives
2 shallots, finely chopped
3 sprigs thyme
2 cups red wine
2 1/2 cups Veal Stock (page 189)
Freshly ground black pepper to taste
Juice of 1/2 lemon

Braised Turnips
1 tablespoon vegetable oil
1 carrot, finely chopped
1 rib celery, finely chopped
1/2 small white or yellow onion, finely chopped
2 cups Chicken Stock (page 186)
1 1/2 cups water
2 extra-large or 3 medium turnips, peeled

Leek-Tomato Sauté
1 tablespoon vegetable oil
3 leeks, white and light green parts only, thinly sliced on the diagonal
6 plum tomatoes, peeled, seeded, and diced
Salt and freshly ground black pepper to taste

Fish
3 tablespoons coarsely cracked white pepper
3 tablespoons coarsely cracked black pepper
6 (6-ounce) Ahi tuna steaks, cut into 3-inch squares about 1-inch thick
1 tablespoon vegetable oil

6 long sprigs of rosemary, leaves stripped from the bottom 2 inches

Crisps. In a food processor, combine the olives and garlic with the olive oil and purée to a very fine consistency, scraping down the sides of the bowl as necessary. Transfer the olive purée to a fine sieve and let drain for about 15 minutes, stirring occasionally. Save the drained oil for a vinaigrette and return the olive purée, which should be very thick, to the food processor. Gradually add the egg yolk, egg, cornmeal, and flour, pulsing the machine and scraping down the sides of the bowl as needed until a soft dough forms. Turn out onto a floured board, cut the dough into 2 equal portions, wrap in plastic wrap, and refrigerate for 1 hour. Using a pasta machine or a rolling pin, roll out one-half of the dough to a 1/16 inch thickness and cut out 6 diamonds. Cut a dime-sized circle out of the center of each diamond. (You will not use the other portion of dough, but it can be stored in the refrigerator for up to 1 week or frozen for later use.)

In a large, heavy saucepan or deep-fryer, heat a generous amount of vegetable oil to 350°. Gently slide the diamonds into the oil and fry until crisp, about $1^1/_2$ minutes. Set aside on a paper towel–lined plate to drain.

Sauce. Finely dice 10 of the olives and set aside. Place the remaining olives, the shallots, thyme sprigs, and red wine in a medium saucepan. Over medium-high heat, bring the wine to a simmer and reduce it by half. Add the stock and again reduce by half, so that a generous $1^1/_2$ cups of slightly syrupy liquid remains. Remove and discard the thyme. Place the mixture in a blender and blend at high speed for about 1 minute, then strain through a fine sieve into a clean saucepan, scraping the sieve to push all the sauce through. Stir in the lemon juice and diced olives and season to taste with pepper. Set aside.

Turnips. Heat a large saucepan over medium-low heat and add the oil. Add the carrot, celery, and onion and sauté until slightly softened, about 2 to 3 minutes. Add the stock and water and increase the heat to bring the mixture to a boil. Add the turnips, then partially cover the pan and lower the heat. Simmer the turnips for 20 minutes, turn them over, and simmer for 15 to 20 minutes more, or until tender. Remove the pan from the heat and let the turnips cool, uncovered, in the stock. (They will continue to cook for a little while in the hot stock, and should be tender but not mushy once cool.) When cool, cut each turnip into 2 or 3 large disks at least $^1/_2$ inch thick (you need 6 large disks). Set aside in a small roasting pan, tightly covered. Reserve the stock and the trimmings for another use.

Sauté. Heat a medium skillet over medium-high heat and add the vegetable oil. Add the leeks and sauté for 2 to 3 minutes, or until softened. Add the tomatoes and sauté for 1 minute more. Add salt and black pepper, remove the pan from the heat, and set aside.

Fish. Combine the white and black cracked pepper and spread them evenly on a small tray. Lightly coat one side of each tuna steak with the pepper by setting it down on the paper, but not pressing the pepper into the flesh. Immediately heat a large skillet over high heat and add the vegetable oil. Sear the steaks, pepper side down, for about 2 minutes, then turn over and cook for $1^1/_2$ to 2 minutes more, depending on how rare you like your tuna.

Assembly. Place a turnip slice in the center of each of 6 heated dinner plates. Cut each tuna steak into 4 equal cubes, then reassemble the cubes into a square on top of each turnip slice with the rare inner sides of the cubes facing outward. Place a small dollop of the leek-tomato mixture on the tuna squares, and top each with an olive crisp. Insert a rosemary sprig through the center of each olive crisp, the leek-tomato mixture, tuna, and turnip slices to hold them all together. Spoon about 2 tablespoons of the sauce around the edge of each plate and serve immediately.

Mark's Phad Thai with Seared Tuna

Yield: 4 servings

Mark Valiani is one of the talented young chefs I've been fortunate enough to work with. When Mark was my chef de cuisine at Röx, in Beverly Hills, he came up with this dish, and it has been on and off my menu ever since. This recipe calls for quite a few specialized Asian ingredients, which are available at Asian markets and specialty stores.

Red Chile Glaze

3 roasted red bell peppers, stemmed, seeded,
  and peeled (page 202)
1½ cups mirin wine
2 tablespoons Sambal Olek chili paste
2 tablespoons heavy cream
2 teaspoons freshly squeezed lime juice
Salt to taste

Sauce

½ cup plus 1 tablespoon sweet soy sauce
2 cloves garlic, finely chopped
1½ tablespoons Sambal Olek chili paste
⅓ cup freshly squeezed lime juice
2 teaspoons grated fresh ginger
⅓ cup Vietnamese fish sauce (nuoc mam)

Noodles

1 pound dried clear rice noodles, soaked
  for 10 minutes in hot water to soften
2 tablespoons peanut oil
1 red bell pepper, stemmed, seeded,
  and cut into ¼-inch julienne
1 cup fresh bean sprouts
1 cup loosely packed fresh cilantro sprigs
3 large eggs, beaten well
½ cup Chicken Stock (page 186)
2 tablespoons cold unsalted butter, cut
  into 4 pieces

Fish

4 (3 x 3-inch) squares of sushi-quality Ahi
  tuna, ½ inch thick
Salt and freshly ground pepper to taste
1 tablespoon vegetable oil

⅓ cup crushed roasted peanuts
⅓ cup finely chopped green onions, white
  and light green parts only

Glaze. In a large saucepan, combine the roasted bell peppers, mirin, and chili paste. Bring the mixture to a gentle simmer over medium-low heat. Simmer until the liquid is almost completely evaporated, about 20 to 25 minutes. Transfer the mixture to a blender, add the cream and blend until smooth. Add the lime juice and salt, transfer to a squirt bottle (see Note) and set aside.

Sauce. In a small saucepan, combine all the sauce ingredients, bring to a boil over medium-high heat and boil for 5 minutes. Remove from the heat and set aside.

Noodles. Drain the soaking rice noodles well. Heat a large, heavy skillet over high heat and add the peanut oil. Add the pepper, bean sprouts, and cilantro and sauté for 1½ minutes, tossing quickly. Pour in the beaten egg and stir for 10 seconds, then add the drained noodles, the sauce, and the stock. Deglaze the pan, stirring and scraping all the flavorful bits from the bottom. Lower the heat to medium-high and simmer the noodles for 5 to 6 minutes, or until most of the liquid has been absorbed. Remove from the heat and stir in the butter until it is all absorbed. Taste, adjust seasonings as necessary, and set aside, covered, while you immediately cook the tuna.

Fish. Season the tuna squares with salt and black pepper. Heat a large, heavy skillet over high heat and add the vegetable oil. When the oil is very hot, add the tuna squares and sear for 30 seconds, then turn over and sear for another 30 seconds. Remove from the heat.

Assembly. Mound an equal amount of the noodle mixture in each of 4 large heated dinner bowls. Top each mound of noodles with a square of seared tuna and sprinkle with some of the peanuts and green onions. Using the squirt bottle, garnish with the glaze, making a zig-zag design over each serving. Serve immediately.

Note: No piece of equipment is more valuable than a squirt bottle for decorating plates with colorful sauces. You can use a recycled mustard squirt bottle or one of the clear bottles sold for this purpose at specialty cookware stores.

Roasted Black Cod in Thai Curry Broth with Steamed Carrots and Potatoes

Yield: 6 servings

When I came to this country I wasn't familiar with many Asian ingredients. Thai flavors were the first ones I tried and I instantly fell in love and started experimenting. After a few minor mishaps, I learned to combine them with my European techniques. You can find the lemongrass, curry paste, and fish sauce at Asian markets.

Thai Curry Broth

2 tablespoons peanut oil

2 green onions, white and light green parts only, finely chopped

2 tablespoons finely chopped fresh cilantro

1 stalk fresh lemongrass, thinly sliced

$1/2$ small yellow onion, finely chopped

2 cloves garlic, finely chopped

Scant tablespoon grated fresh ginger

2 lime leaves, finely sliced

$1^{1}/_{2}$ cups Chicken Stock (page 186)

$3/4$ cup canned coconut milk

$1/2$ cup half-and-half

1 tablespoon Vietnamese fish sauce (nuoc nam)

2 teaspoons soy sauce

2 teaspoons freshly squeezed lime juice

Tiny pinch of saffron threads

1 tablespoon sugar

2 teaspoons Thai curry paste

Vegetables

$1/2$ pound white or red rose potatoes, peeled and cut into 1-inch chunks

$1/2$ pound small carrots, peeled and cut $3/8$ inch thick on the diagonal

Fish

6 (6-ounce) pieces boneless black or rock cod

Salt and freshly ground black pepper

1 tablespoon vegetable oil

2 leeks, white parts only, cut into 2 x $1/8$-inch julienne and deep-fried, for garnish (page 202)

Broth. Heat a large, heavy saucepan over medium-high heat and add the peanut oil. Add the green onions, cilantro, lemongrass, onion, garlic, ginger, and lime leaves and sauté, tossing occasionally, for 2 to 3 minutes, or until the mixture is glossy and slightly softened. Add the chicken stock, coconut milk, half-and-half, fish sauce, soy sauce, lime juice, saffron, and sugar and deglaze the pan, stirring and scraping all the flavorful bits from the bottom and sides. Bring the liquid to a rapid simmer and reduce to $3/4$ of its volume, then stir in the curry paste. Strain the mixture into a clean pan, pressing firmly on the solids to extract all the liquid, then discard the solids. Cover and set aside.

Vegetables. Bring a medium saucepan of lightly salted water to a boil. Add the potatoes and cook for 10 to 15 minutes, or until tender. Remove the potatoes with a slotted spoon, drain, transfer them to a clean, dry pan, and cover. Add the carrots to the boiling water and cook until tender, about 8 to 10 minutes. Drain the carrots well and combine them with the potatoes. Cover and set aside.

Fish. Preheat the oven to 375° and place a roasting pan inside to heat. Season the cod with salt and black pepper. Heat a large, heavy skillet over high heat and add the vegetable oil. Add the cod pieces and sear for about 3 minutes on each side, then transfer them to the roasting pan. Place in the oven to finish cooking, about 6 to 8 minutes, or until done through and opaque.

Assembly. While the cod finishes cooking, reheat the curry broth just until hot. Remove the cod pieces from the oven and blot gently with paper towels to remove the cooking oil. Place a piece of fish in the bottom of each of 6 heated dinner bowls and pour an equal amount of the hot broth into each bowl. Surround the cod with the potatoes and carrots and garnish with the deep-fried leeks.

Note: This soup can be a first course for ten (just divide the fish into ten $3^{1}/_{2}$-ounce pieces) or a meal for six.

Growing up in a Restaurant Family

When I was about eight years old, my father, who was a butcher, started working in various restaurants on the weekend to train himself to run a top-quality restaurant. I was about ten years old when my parents opened their restaurant. In the old days, butcher shops and restaurants often went together—one was just a natural offshoot of the other—so my father already had many of the basic cooking skills. He knew how to make superb sauces and, of course, he had a great understanding of all meats.

I certainly wouldn't say that I had an instant affinity for cooking and good food. Before the restaurant opened, my dad would bring home the best cuts of meat and then complain that my sister and I didn't appreciate them. Nevertheless, I was exposed to exotic flavors and textures such as those of tripe (which I refused to eat) and learned about foods, especially meat, without really meaning to—it was just part of my life. So, by the time I was about twelve, I knew what was good and what was not, not just based on flavor but on texture and my general knowledge of food.

Before we had the restaurant, we were not very well off, and my mother was not a particularly good cook. My father only cooked on the weekends and, though he always made something special for Sunday lunch, our diet was basically simple. But once we opened the restaurant, I was immersed in a whole different level of cooking. Of course I had to help, because there was a lot of work to do. When my friends were playing soccer after school and on the weekends, I was mixing up batches of spätzle. In fact, it was a bit of a sore point between my father and me. I saw how hard my parents worked, and at a certain point I didn't want to cook or to be in the kitchen.

By the time I was fifteen or sixteen, however, my friends and I were deciding what careers to pursue and applying for apprenticeships or further schooling. In Germany, you have to decide what course you want your life to take when you are still in your teens, and all I knew was that I wanted to be independent. Further schooling would have meant more years at home. It is possible to change one's mind and try another career, but in Germany you don't just fall into a career—you train for it, take exams, and then become certified. Everyone must earn the right to be called a chef, a butcher, a carpenter, or whatever by meeting the established requirements. Sometime during those years, I realized I really enjoyed cooking when I wasn't doing it as part of my family chores. My decision wasn't based on any great intuition or demonstration of extraordinary talent—I just thought I should give cooking a try since I already had a solid base of knowledge. So, I enrolled in one of the standard intensive three-year classical internship and training courses. This wasn't an unusual commitment—60 or 70 percent of Germany's young adults complete this type of training in various vocations. Once I neared the end of my training, I knew I'd made the right decision and came to know firsthand the sense of accomplishment and personal satisfaction my parents must have felt when they took up the restaurant life.

Medallions of Norwegian Salmon with a Smoked Salmon and Horseradish Topping

Yield: 6 servings

This harmonious, elegant, and visually stunning dish harkens back to my "nouvelle cuisine" days. The smoked and fresh salmon, horseradish, and creamy beurre blanc make a perfect quartet. This dish is actually easier to prepare than it may sound. The key is to ask your butcher for 2 whole perfect fillet sections of salmon, as specified. Note that the beurre blanc cannot be reheated, so it should be made just before the fish is cooked.

Medallions

1½ pounds center-cut Norwegian salmon, skin and all central bones removed, cut through the backbone into 2 whole fillets

Topping

4 (1-inch-thick) slices white French bread, crusts removed and cut into 1-inch cubes

½ teaspoon wasabi powder

7 ounces smoked salmon (irregular cuts are fine)

2 tablespoons prepared horseradish

Juice of 1 large lemon

Pinch of ground cayenne pepper

6 tablespoons cold unsalted butter, cut into 12 pieces

2 cups warm Beurre Blanc (page 38)

2 teaspoons vegetable oil

½ teaspoon salt

36 asparagus tips

18 Home-Cured Tomatoes (page 186)

Medallions. Cut each fillet section into 6 equal slices. Take 2 slices of salmon fillet and place the thicker rounded end of one against the thinner end of the other as if you were lining up 2 shoes, heel to toe. Wrap the ends around to meet each other, to form a circle that is as round as possible. (If you can make a rounder circle by fitting the pieces together differently, do so.) Skewer the medallions with two toothpicks, one inserted into each rounded side until they meet in the center, and secure well (the medallions will firm up as soon as they begin to cook). Repeat with the remaining fillets until you have 6 medallions. Cover and refrigerate.

Topping. In the bowl of a food processor, place the bread cubes and wasabi powder and pulse several times to mix. Add the smoked salmon, horseradish, lemon juice, and cayenne. Pulse the machine on and off, scraping down the sides of the bowl as necessary, until the mixture is crumbly. Add the butter and pulse until it is well combined, again scraping the bowl as necessary. Turn the paste out onto a 13-inch-long sheet of plastic wrap and cover it with another 13-inch-long sheet. Working quickly so that the butter doesn't get too soft, roll or press the mixture gently into an 11 x 11-inch square that is ¼ inch thick. Peel off the top sheet of plastic wrap and place the salmon medallions on top of the paste. Cut around each medallion so that a disk of the topping adheres to the fish, then lift it with a metal spatula and place topping side up on a tray. Refrigerate while you prepare the beurre blanc. Gather the remaining topping into a ball and refrigerate or freeze for another use.

Assembly. Preheat a broiler to high. Heat a large, heavy ovenproof skillet over medium-high heat, then add the vegetable oil and sprinkle the salt evenly over the base of the pan. Immediately add the salmon medallions, topping side up, and place under the hot broiler. Cook until the topping is crusty and brown, about 6 to 7 minutes, turning the pan as needed to make sure the topping browns evenly, then remove from the heat and let the medallions rest in the pan for 5 minutes. Bring a pan of water to a boil. Add the asparagus tips and blanch for 6 minutes. Remove with a skimmer, shock in ice water, then drain on paper towels.

Place a salmon medallion in the center of each of 6 heated dinner plates. Spoon a generous amount of beurre blanc around the edge of each plate. Arrange three separate pairs of asparagus tips equidistant around each medallion, radiating outward like a wagon wheel. Set a home-cured tomato between each pair of asparagus tips and serve immediately.

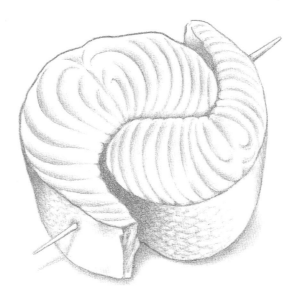

Roasted Quail with Pomegranate Reduction and Bread and Bacon Stuffing on Bitter Greens

Yield: 6 servings

When selecting quail, look for plump, fresh birds with pink and white skin and red flesh. Any gray coloration can mean that they have been frozen and have oxidized to some degree. Ask the butcher to remove the bones for you. For a more substantial main course, serve 2 quail per person. This is a wonderful fall dish.

Pomegranate Reduction
3 cups fresh pomegranate juice (see Note)

Dressing
1 tablespoon Thai curry paste
¼ cup freshly squeezed lemon juice
½ teaspoon salt
¼ teaspoon freshly ground black pepper
½ cup olive oil

Quail
3 thick slices bacon, cut into small dice
2 carrots, cut into ¼-inch dice
1 yellow onion, cut into ¼-inch dice
3 ribs celery, cut into ¼-inch dice
3 small cloves garlic, finely chopped
1½ teaspoons cumin seed
Salt and freshly ground black pepper to taste
3 cups mixed rye, multigrain, and
  corn bread croutons
6 boneless quail

3 tablespoons vegetable oil
6 cups (about 6 ounces) loosely
  packed mixed bitter baby greens
2 tablespoons Curry Oil (page 199)

continued

Roasted Quail *continued*

Reduction. In a medium nonreactive saucepan, reduce the pomegranate juice over medium heat to one-quarter of its original volume, until only about 3/4 cup of syrupy liquid remains. Set aside.

Dressing. In a small mixing bowl, whisk together the curry paste, lemon juice, salt, and pepper. Gradually whisk in the olive oil until emulsified, then whisk for 1 minute more. Cover and set aside. (Both the reduction and dressing may be made up to 24 hours in advance.)

Quail. In a large, nonstick skillet, sauté the bacon until it is browned and crisp. Drain off and discard the excess fat from the pan. Add the carrots, onion, and celery to the pan and stir over medium heat for 5 minutes more, or until the vegetables are softened. Add the garlic, cumin, salt, and pepper and sauté for 1 minute more. Transfer to a mixing bowl and toss thoroughly with the croutons, then set aside to cool completely.

Rinse and pat the quail dry with paper towels then stuff loosely with the cooled stuffing and truss with kitchen twine.

Preheat the oven to 375° and place a roasting pan inside to heat. In a very large skillet, heat the vegetable oil over medium-high heat and sear three of the quail on all sides, turning with tongs to make sure they brown evenly, about 5 to 7 minutes. Repeat for the remaining quail. When all of the quail are browned, transfer them to the roasting pan to finish cooking, about 7 to 8 minutes more, or until firm and the juices from the thigh run pale pink.

Assembly. Gently reheat the Pomegranate Reduction over low heat. In a large mixing bowl, toss the baby greens with the dressing and mound an equal amount on each of 6 serving plates. Place a quail in the center of the greens and drizzle the reduction over the quail and the salad. Drizzle 2 teaspoons of the Curry Oil around the edges of the plate and serve at once.

Note: Fresh pomegranate juice can be found at farmers' markets and some health food stores. If unavailable fresh, it is also sold jarred and frozen in some gourmet markets.

Lamb Loin with a Tarragon Crust and Red Wine Sauce

Yield: 6 servings

Tarragon is a bold, strongly flavored herb; that's why for this dish you will want to find a good butcher who still carries the kind of lamb that tastes like lamb, not the lamb that is bred to have a mild, non-gamey flavor. For a time, we got our lamb from a purveyor in New Mexico—it had that slightly salty, gamey flavor that the French salt-marsh-raised lamb has. Unfortunately, we had to switch to another supplier, but I maintain the search for real lamb.

Tarragon Crust

Two ¹/₂-inch-thick slices brioche, or other rich egg bread, crusts removed, cut into ¹/₂-inch cubes

¹/₂ cup loosely packed flat-leaf parsley leaves

2 tablespoons loosely packed fresh tarragon leaves

¹/₂ cup loosely packed chervil

¹/₄ teaspoon salt

Freshly ground black pepper to taste

2 tablespoons cold unsalted butter, cut into 4 pieces

Lamb

1 tablespoon olive oil

2 (10-ounce) lamb loins

Salt and freshly ground black pepper to taste

3 cups Red Wine Sauce (page 195)

Crust. In a food processor, pulse the bread several times until you have fine bread crumbs. Add the parsley, tarragon, chervil, salt, and pepper, then process until the mixture is evenly mixed and crumbly. Add the butter and process again until the mixture clumps slightly. Place a large rectangle of parchment paper on the work surface and turn the crust mixture out onto it.

Spread the crumbs into a 4 x 4-inch square. Place a large sheet of plastic wrap on top and, with a rolling pin, roll out the mixture into a flat 8 x 8-inch sheet about ¹/₈ inch thick. Fold over the edges of the plastic wrap and seal, so that the edges of the crust don't dry out. Refrigerate for 1 hour.

Lamb. Heat a large skillet over medium-high heat and add the olive oil. Season the lamb loins with salt and pepper, then add to the skillet and sauté for about 1 minute on each of all 4 sides (the lamb should still be very pink in the middle). Cool the lamb for 15 minutes on a wire rack resting over a baking sheet to catch any juices.

Preheat the oven to 450° and place a lightly oiled roasting pan inside to heat. Preheat a broiler to high heat. Remove the plastic wrap from the crust and place the lamb loins on top. Press the loins down firmly onto the crust, then cut around each piece so that the crust can be lifted off with the lamb. (You may need to lift the crust with the knife and then press it gently back into place.)

Set the lamb loins crust side up in the roasting pan and place in the oven for about 4 minutes to finish cooking. Transfer the pan to the hot broiler for 4 minutes to crisp the crust (it will remain bright green). Cool for 5 minutes.

Assembly. Carefully slice the lamb loins into ³/₄-inch slices and place 3 slices on each of 6 heated serving plates. Drizzle some of the Red Wine Sauce around the edge of the plates and serve immediately.

Stuffed Free-Range Chicken with Parsnip Pancakes and Applesauce

Yield: 6 servings

This is an updated version of a traditional dish called "Veal Cordon Bleu," which my father used to serve in our family restaurant when I was a child. I wanted a lighter dish, so I substituted chicken for the veal and dispensed with the breading. And the goat cheese I've added contributes a much more intense flavor than the traditional Swiss. In fact, I think it has become a completely different dish!

▶ Applesauce

3 Granny Smith apples, peeled, cored, and cut into ½-inch cubes

3 McIntosh apples, peeled, cored, and cut into ½-inch cubes

½ cup sugar

Juice of 1 lemon

4 tablespoons unsalted butter

1 teaspoon ground cinnamon

Parsnip Pancakes

1½ large parsnips (8 to 10 ounces total), peeled

½ cup all-purpose flour

½ small yellow onion, very finely chopped

½ teaspoon salt

Freshly ground white pepper to taste

1 egg, lightly beaten

Chicken

6 single boneless, skinless free-range chicken breasts, with the wing bones still attached (about 7 ounces each)

6 ounces soft goat cheese

6 large thin slices of cooked ham

Salt and freshly ground white pepper to taste

¼ cup olive oil

2 tablespoons unsalted butter

Applesauce. In a large saucepan, combine all the ingredients over medium-low heat and cover. Stirring occasionally, cook the apples until they are softened but not broken down, 25 to 35 minutes. Cover and set aside.

Pancakes. Bring a medium saucepan of lightly salted water to a boil. Add the parsnips and blanch for 10 to 12 minutes, or until almost tender. Drain the parsnips very well, pat dry with paper towels, and coarsely grate into a large bowl. Add the flour, onion, salt, and white pepper and combine well. Stir in the egg and mix until a thick batter forms. Lightly flour your hands and form the mixture into six 3-inch patties. Set aside, covered with a kitchen towel, on a very lightly floured plate.

Chicken. Butterfly the chicken breasts by carefully cutting a pocket lengthwise in one edge of each chicken breast. Divide the goat cheese into 6 equal portions and roll each one inside a slice of ham into a long, thin tube. Tuck the tube of ham in the pocket. Secure the seam of the pocket with 3 or 4 toothpicks. Season the chicken breasts with salt and white pepper.

Preheat the oven to 425° and place a roasting pan inside to heat. Heat a large skillet over medium-high heat and add 2 tablespoons of the olive oil. Add the chicken breasts and sauté, in 2 batches if necessary, until golden, about 10 minutes, turning with tongs so that both sides brown evenly. Transfer the chicken to the roasting pan and finish cooking for 8 to 10 minutes more, or until cooked through with no trace of pink remaining.

Assembly. While the chicken finishes cooking, heat a large nonstick skillet over medium-low heat. Add the remaining 2 tablespoons of olive oil and the butter. Add the parsnip pancakes and cook slowly, turning them over when the bottom is golden and crisp. They will take 4 to 5 minutes on each side.

Place a pancake on one side of each of 6 heated serving plates and place a dollop of applesauce next to it. Remove the toothpicks from the chicken breasts and cut each in half, crosswise on the diagonal. Arrange the two halves opposite the pancakes on each plate and serve immediately.

Roasted Leg of Rabbit Stuffed with a Basil-Wrapped Rabbit Tenderloin with Couscous Salad

Yield: 6 servings

In this beautiful dish, the rabbit tenderloin remains juicy and delicately moist because it is protected by the sturdier leg meat surrounding it. As you slice it, you'll see the basil-wrapped tenderloin inside. Boning a rabbit leg is a little tricky the first time, although it's not as difficult as you might imagine. If you don't want to tackle the task, just ask your butcher to do it for you.

The couscous salad makes enough for 8 servings, but you'll be glad to have some left over. If you can't find the large-grain couscous (also called "osem" or Israeli roasted pasta), which is available in Middle Eastern markets, just substitute the same amount of medium-grain quick-cooking couscous.

Couscous Salad
1 tablespoon vegetable oil
¹/₂ small yellow onion, finely diced
¹/₂ teaspoon turmeric
8.8 ounces large-grain couscous
2 to 2¹/₂ cups water
¹/₂ green zucchini, quartered lengthwise
¹/₂ yellow zucchini, quartered lengthwise
¹/₂ red bell pepper, stemmed and seeded
2¹/₂ tablespoons extra virgin olive oil
1 tablespoon finely chopped flat-leaf parsley
3 tablespoons freshly squeezed lemon juice
¹/₂ teaspoon salt
Freshly ground black pepper to taste

Rabbit
6 large rabbit legs (including thighs and
   drumsticks), boned
6 rabbit tenderloins
24 large leaves basil
Salt and cracked black pepper to taste
1 tablespoon clarified butter (page 202)

2 cups mâche, optional
¹/₄ cup Balsamic Vinaigrette (page 193)
¹/₃ cup Basil Pesto Sauce (page 196), thinned
   with 1 tablespoon olive oil

Salad. Heat a large, heavy saucepan over medium heat and add the vegetable oil. Add the onion and sauté for 3 to 4 minutes, or until softened, and then stir in the turmeric. Add the couscous and stir for about 3 minutes, or until the grains are coated and just beginning to brown. Add ¹/₂ cup of the water and continue to stir while the couscous simmers. Continue stirring and adding water until the couscous is tender. (You may not need all of the water.) The process will only take a few minutes. Immediately spread the couscous on a tray and fluff with a fork. Let cool to room temperature.

Preheat a grill or broiler to high heat. Lay the zucchini quarters skin side down on the work surface. Carefully trim away the triangle of inner core, leaving only the peel with about ¹/₄-inch of flesh still attached. Brush the zucchini and the bell pepper with 1 tablespoon of the olive oil. Grill the vegetables until slightly charred on both sides. When cool, cut into ¹/₂-inch-wide strips and then cut the strips crosswise on the diagonal into ¹/₂-inch diamonds. In a medium mixing bowl, combine the chilled couscous with the vegetables, the remaining 1¹/₂ tablespoons olive oil, the parsley, and lemon juice. Stir in the salt and pepper.

Rabbit. Place a rabbit leg on the work surface with the fleshy, thick side down. With your fingertips, locate the thigh bone. Make a deep

continued

Roasted Leg of Rabbit *continued*

cut along the bone, carefully cutting through the joint that attaches it to the drumstick without cutting all the way through and severing the two parts of the leg. Scraping and trimming away the flesh, remove the thigh bone, being careful not to cut through to the other side of the thigh. "Butterfly" the thigh by making a few shallow cuts in the flesh on either side and flattening it out. Cut 1 of the loins in half and place the narrow end against the wide one, to form a fairly even cylinder. Wrap the cylinder with 4 basil leaves and tuck it inside the thigh cavity. Bring the sides of the thigh meat up and over to enclose the loin and, using 4 pieces of kitchen twine, tie firmly but not tightly in 4 places. Repeat the process with the other 5 legs.

Preheat the oven to 350° and place a roasting pan inside to heat. Season the rabbit legs with salt and cracked pepper. Heat a large, heavy skillet over medium-high heat and add the clarified butter. Add the stuffed legs and sauté for about 3 minutes on each side, or until golden, then transfer them to the pan in the oven. Roast the legs for 15 to 20 minutes, or until the thigh juices run clear. Let rest for 5 minutes.

Assembly. In a small bowl, toss the mâche with the vinaigrette until evenly coated. Slice each rabbit thigh crosswise into $1/2$-inch-wide slices and fan them out with the drumstick at one end. Place on one side of the plate. Place a mound of the couscous salad on the other side of the plate. Make small mound of mâche leaves by the salad and drizzle pesto sauce next to the rabbit.

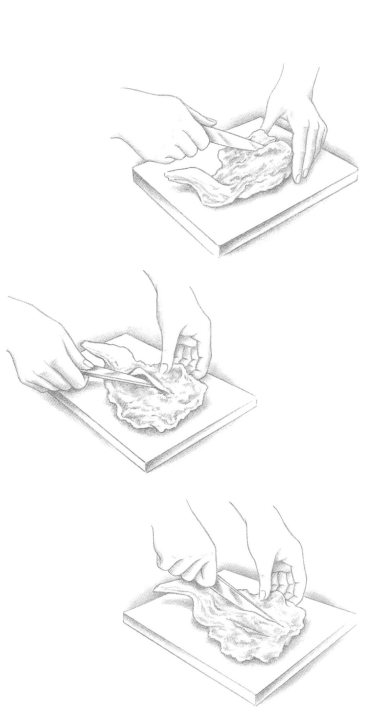

A Cold-Smoking Primer

The aim of cold-smoking meats, fish, or vegetables is to impart a subtle smoky flavor without cooking the ingredients. Cold-smoked fish and vegetables can be eaten without cooking, but all meats and game must be cooked. Virginia ham, lox, bacon, and many fresh sausages are cold-smoked.

Cold-smoking is done at a temperature between 90° and 130°; higher temperatures will cook, not smoke, the food. Many home smokers are on the market now, and barbecue retailers usually stock at least one type. These inexpensive, uncomplicated devices work by keeping their contents at a constant temperature in a smoke-filled, fireproof chamber. Because it is difficult to regulate the temperature of a charcoal smoker for any length of time, most of my friends use electric smokers. If you have a place to use a smoker outside, I highly recommend purchasing one. Plan to experiment a bit to determine exactly what level of smokiness you prefer.

Follow the smoker manufacturer's instructions for cold-smoking, using sawdust (not wood chunks), which will continue to smolder at a low temperature. The sawdust should be soaked in water for several hours and then drained before being placed in the smoking pan. If you have trouble maintaining a low enough temperature in a charcoal, gas, or electric water smoker, add ice cubes to the water pan. Be sure to use a thermometer with a long sensor wand that extends to the cooking rack level and is visible through the top of the smoker so you can check the temperature regularly. Keep the air vents just slightly open so that you can see the comforting thread of smoke rising from the top. This will let you know if the sawdust embers have ceased smoldering, in which case you will need to increase the heat briefly to reignite the coals.

All meats, seafood, and vegetables can be cold-smoked. When smoking meats, keep in mind that the fattier cuts are best as they tend to absorb and retain more of the smoky flavor. Smoking times are based solely on the size and weight of the ingredients and the cook's personal taste. I once over-smoked a fish so badly it was inedible. In such a case, nothing can be done to salvage the food; you must start over. If you under-smoke an ingredient, you can either resmoke it or make a note to increase the smoking time on your next try. Keeping detailed records of all your attempts is the best way to master the technique.

Roasted Cornish Hens with Wilted Greens and Lentils

Yield: 6 servings

You'll need a home smoker to prepare this dish. Just follow the manufacturer's instructions for cold-smoking, a process that imparts a lovely smoky flavor without actually cooking the food. (For more about smoking, see page 119.) Making the stock is fairly time consuming (though well worth it), so you'll want to make it a day or two before you plan to serve the dish. I may be old-fashioned, but I still believe that presoaking lentils makes them cook more evenly. You may want to make these lentils a regular part of your cooking repertoire.

You can get the chicken carcasses and breast bones from your butcher shop—most butchers have plenty of them left over from preparing boneless chicken breasts.

Smoked Chicken Stock
3 uncooked chicken carcasses, or about
  2¹/₂ pounds breast bones
2 tablespoons vegetable oil
¹/₂ large yellow onion, coarsely chopped
2 carrots, coarsely chopped
1 rib celery, coarsely chopped
1 cup dry red wine
4 cups Chicken Stock (page 186)
10 to 12 cups water
1 teaspoon salt
¹/₂ teaspoon freshly ground black pepper
1 bay leaf

Lentils
2 teaspoons olive oil
¹/₄ cup finely diced yellow onions
¹/₄ cup finely diced carrots
1 small rib celery, finely diced
1¹/₂ cups French green lentils, soaked in cold
  water to cover for 30 minutes
Smoked Chicken Stock
¹/₂ teaspoon salt
Freshly ground black pepper to taste
1 tablespoon balsamic vinegar

Hens
6 small Cornish game hens, rinsed and dried
³/₄ cup unsalted butter, softened
3 cloves garlic, finely chopped
2 teaspoons finely chopped fresh thyme
1 teaspoon salt
¹/₂ teaspoon freshly ground black pepper

Greens
2 tablespoons vegetable oil
6 cups (about 6 ounces) loosely packed baby
  mustard greens, arugula, dandelion greens,
  or any mixture of bitter baby greens

6 toasted Focaccia Bread wedges,
  for garnish (page 145)

Stock. Prepare a smoker for cold-smoking, using a generous amount of well-soaked sawdust. Smoke the raw chicken carcasses, undisturbed, for 30 minutes.

Preheat the oven to 375°. Swirl the oil in a large roasting pan. Add the chicken carcasses and the vegetables and roast in the oven for about 45 minutes, turning the ingredients over twice during the cooking time. Transfer the bones and vegetables to a large stockpot and discard any fat remaining in the roasting pan, leaving the roasting juices. Deglaze the pan with the red wine, stirring and scraping all the flavorful bits from the bottom and sides of the pan, then pour the wine into the stockpot. Add the chicken stock and water to cover the ingredients by 1 inch. Bring the liquid to a simmer and skim off any impurities that rise to the surface, then simmer slowly for 30 minutes. Add the salt, pepper, and bay leaf and simmer for 1 1/2 hours more.

Strain the stock through a colander lined with a double thickness of slightly dampened cheesecloth, pressing firmly on the solids to extract all the remaining liquid. Discard the solids. Transfer the stock to a clean saucepan and reduce to one-third of the original volume. The stock can be made up to 2 days in advance, covered, and refrigerated until you are ready to finish the recipe. Any extra stock can be frozen for up to 3 months.

Lentils. Heat a large, heavy saucepan over medium-low heat and add the olive oil. Add the onions, carrots, and celery and sauté, stirring occasionally, for 2 to 3 minutes, or until softened. Add the lentils and sauté for 1 minute more. Add enough Smoked Chicken Stock to cover the lentils by 2 inches. Bring the liquid to a simmer, cover partially, and cook for 25 to 30 minutes, or until the lentils are tender but not mushy. Stir in the salt, pepper, and balsamic vinegar. The mixture should have a saucelike consistency. Cover and set aside.

Hens. Preheat the oven to 375°. Rub the hens all over and inside the cavity with the softened butter. Combine the garlic, thyme, salt, and pepper together and sprinkle over the hens, making sure to coat all sides evenly. Truss the legs firmly to keep the hens compact, and arrange them on a rack in a roasting pan large enough to hold them all with space between each one. Roast for 35 to 40 minutes, or until the thigh juices run clear.

Greens. Meanwhile, heat a large, heavy skillet over medium-high heat and add the vegetable oil. Add the greens and sauté for up to 10 minutes, tossing every 2 minutes. (The cooking time will depend on the type and the maturity of the greens; they should be cooked until tender.)

Assembly. Place a mound of the greens in the center of each of 6 heated dinner plates and spoon some of the lentils around the edges. Perch a roasted hen on top of each mound of greens. Lean 1 wedge of focaccia against each hen and serve immediately.

Beef Tenderloins with Goat Cheese
Mashed Potatoes, Thyme Crisps, and Red Wine Sauce

Yield: 6 servings

This dish remains one of the top sellers at the restaurant. It's basically meat and potatoes (with a twist), and will appeal to all steak lovers. The red wine sauce is rich and unctuous and the potatoes are so addictive we should probably put a warning on the menu. This is one of several recipes in the book that is easier if you own a mandoline, a tool for slicing thinly and evenly. Expensive models are available from gourmet equipment retailers, but Japanese restaurant-supply stores sell a wonderful plastic version for a fraction of the price.

Thyme Crisps
¼ cup unsalted butter, melted
Salt
Freshly ground white pepper
2 very large or 3 medium russet potatoes
1½ tablespoons fresh thyme leaves

3 cups Red Wine Sauce (page 195)

Mashed Potatoes
4 russet potatoes (about 8 ounces each), peeled
   and quartered
½ to ¾ cup milk
½ cup unsalted butter
½ teaspoon salt
Freshly ground white pepper to taste
⅔ cup soft goat cheese

Vegetables
1½ teaspoons vegetable oil
12 small shallots
1½ teaspoons coarsely cracked black pepper
¼ teaspoon salt
9 thin spears asparagus, cut into 3-inch lengths
1½ carrots, cut into 2 x ¼-inch julienne
1½ medium parsnips, or 1 large turnip, cut into
   2 x ½-inch batons

Tenderloins
1 tablespoon vegetable oil
Salt and freshly ground black pepper to taste
6 (6-ounce) beef tenderloins

1 tablespoon vegetable oil

Crisps. Preheat the oven to 250°. Line a large baking sheet with parchment paper, brush it with some of the melted butter and sprinkle with salt and white pepper. Cut the potatoes into large rectangular blocks, saving the trimmings for another use. Using a mandoline or very sharp knife, cut 36 paper-thin rectangular sheets of potato. Lay 18 potato sheets on the buttered parchment and sprinkle some thyme evenly over each sheet, then lay another potato sheet on top of each one. Brush the sheets with butter and sprinkle with salt and pepper. Lay another piece of parchment paper over the potatoes. Place a second large baking sheet on top (to keep the sheets flat) and bake in the warm oven for about 1 hour, or until the potato sheets are deep golden and very crisp. Set aside, uncovered.

Sauce. In a small saucepan over medium-high heat, reduce the sauce to two-thirds of its original volume, about 2 cups. Set aside.

Potatoes. Bring a large saucepan of lightly salted water to a boil. Add the potatoes and cook, uncovered, for about 20 minutes, or until they are very soft. Drain the potatoes well and transfer to a double boiler over gently simmering water. Add the milk, butter, salt, and white pepper. Mash together until smooth, then add the goat cheese and blend until well mixed. Cover the pan, remove from the heat, and set aside.

continued

Beef Tenderloins *continued*

Vegetables. Preheat the oven to 350°. In a large, heavy ovenproof skillet (preferably cast iron) heat the vegetable oil over medium-high heat and sauté the shallots for 2 to 3 minutes, or until softened. Add the cracked pepper and salt. Sauté for 2 minutes more, then transfer the pan to the oven and roast the shallots, stirring occasionally, for 15 to 20 minutes, or until dry and golden. Set aside in a small bowl and wipe out the skillet with a paper towel.

Bring a large saucepan of lightly salted water to a boil. Add the asparagus and blanch for 2 minutes, or until al dente. Using a skimmer, transfer them to a paper towel–lined tray to drain. Add the carrots to the stockpot and blanch for 3 minutes, then remove and drain on the paper towels. Add the parsnips to the stockpot and blanch for 3 to 4 minutes, or until al dente, and drain.

Tenderloins. Over high heat, heat the skillet the shallots were cooked in and add the vegetable oil. Season the tenderloins and sear for 3 minutes on each side for medium-rare, or until done to your liking. Transfer the tenderloins to a warm platter to rest, covered loosely.

Assembly. Again wipe out the skillet with a paper towel, and return the pan to medium-high heat. Add the remaining tablespoon of vegetable oil and the blanched asparagus, carrots, parsnips, and roasted shallots and toss until they are just heated through. If the mashed potatoes are no longer warm, reheat them gently, stirring continuously.

Spoon a mound of mashed potato onto the center of each of 6 large heated serving plates and slightly flatten the top to make a thick disc about $1^1/_2$ inches larger than the diameter of the tenderloins. Place a tenderloin on the mashed potato discs and top with some of the vegetables. Stand 3 thyme crisps upright in the edges of the mashed potato disc. Drizzle the red wine sauce around the mashed potato and vegetables and serve immediately.

Beef and Mushroom Ragout with Spätzle

Yield: 6 servings

Where I come from, spätzle is a rustic pasta dumpling used as a foil for a huge variety of dishes. Once found mostly in the Black Forest/Schwabian region of Germany, it now appears all over the country. In fact, it is probably as ubiquitous as potatoes are in Russia. This is an easy, warm, comforting dish that reflects my humble roots, and it is probably the very first dish I ever cooked from scratch—some 25 years ago!

You can use wild mushrooms in this dish, but because it's a basic, homey dish, white mushrooms work just fine. Beef tenderloin scraps are often less expensive than larger cuts, but you can use a larger piece if scraps are unavailable.

Ragout

2 tablespoons vegetable oil

1 pound, 2 ounces beef tenderloin scraps, cut into approximately ³/₄ x 1¹/₂-inch strips

¹/₂ pound white button mushrooms, sliced ¹/₄ inch thick (about 4 cups)

1 teaspoon Dijon-style mustard

3 tablespoons heavy cream

¹/₂ teaspoon salt

Freshly ground black pepper to taste

1 cup Veal Demiglace (page 188)

1 recipe Spätzle (page 180), hot

4 scallions, white and light green parts only, sliced ¹/₄-inch thick on the diagonal

Ragout. Place a large, heavy skillet over high heat. When it is very hot, add the vegetable oil. Add the beef strips and sauté, tossing frequently, for about 2 minutes, or until seared. Add the mushrooms and cook for 3 to 4 minutes more, tossing, until they give up their liquid. Add the mustard, cream, salt, a generous amount of pepper, and the demiglace. Stir to mix thoroughly and remove from the heat.

Assembly. Make a bed of spätzle in each of 6 heated shallow bowls and top with a generous spoonful of the ragout. Garnish with a few scallions and serve immediately.

Poached Spinach-Stuffed Lamb Loin
with Tomato Fondue and Thyme-Lemon Jus

Yield: 6 servings

Before my dad became a chef, he was a butcher for twenty years. He's the one who turned me on to the classic butcher's dish Boeuf a la Ficelle, *or "beef on a string." Here's the story behind the dish: When a cow was butchered in the old days, a pot of rich broth was made up from all the parts of the cow that weren't sold. As the broth simmered on the butcher shop stove, sausages and hams were poached in it primarily because most butchers did not have skillets, sauté pans, or roasting ovens in their "kitchens." As you can imagine, the broth became extremely flavorful. When the butcher wanted to cook a special dish for his family or regular customers, he would poach a beef tenderloin or another tender cut in the broth, tying the meat to the stockpot with a string for easy raising and lowering. Hence the name of this classic dish. Naturally, my version is just a little different.*

Lamb

2 (10-ounce) lamb loins

1 tablespoon vegetable oil

2 cloves garlic, finely chopped

6 cups (about 6 ounces) loosely packed fresh
   spinach leaves, well washed and shaken dry

Thyme-Lemon Jus

1¹/₂ tablespoons vegetable oil

4 shallots, thinly sliced

3 cloves garlic, thinly sliced

3 sprigs thyme

4 cups Lamb or Beef Stock (page 187)

¹/₂ teaspoon salt

¹/₄ teaspoon freshly ground black pepper

Dash of Tabasco sauce

Juice of 1 lemon or more to taste

Tomato Fondue

10 plum tomatoes, peeled and seeded

1 tablespoon olive oil

1 tablespoon finely chopped garlic

1 tablespoon finely chopped shallot

1 bay leaf

¹/₂ teaspoon salt

Freshly ground black pepper

1 teaspoon finely chopped fresh thyme

15 cups Beef Stock (page 187) or canned
   beef consommé

Lamb. Cut the lamb loins nearly all the way through lengthwise to create a long pocket that will hold the stuffing. Set aside.

Heat a large skillet over medium-low heat and add the vegetable oil. Add the garlic and spinach (all at once), cover, and cook for 2 minutes. Remove the lid and toss the spinach so that the cooked leaves from the bottom are on top, then cover and repeat two more times until all the spinach is tender. Remove from the pan and drain in a colander. When cool enough to handle, squeeze as much liquid out of the spinach as possible and chop coarsely. Divide in half and pack one-half of the spinach into the pocket of each lamb loin. Push the spinach to the center so that the long edges of the loin meet each other, then, pressing the loin together tightly, tie crosswise at 1-inch intervals. Cover and refrigerate for up to 2 hours.

Jus. In a heavy, medium saucepan, heat the vegetable oil over medium-low heat. Add the shallots, garlic, and thyme and sauté, stirring occasionally, for about 10 minutes, or until translucent. Add the stock and bring the liquid to a moderate simmer. Reduce to two-thirds of its original volume, about 3 cups, then add the salt, pepper, Tabasco, and lemon juice. Taste, adust the seasonings as necessary, then remove the thyme sprigs. Cover and set aside.

Fondue. In a food processor, process the tomatoes into a slightly chunky purée. Heat a medium skillet over medium-low heat and add the olive oil. Add the tomatoes, garlic, shallots, and bay leaf and sauté for 8 to 10 minutes, stirring occasionally, until thickened. Add the salt, pepper, and thyme, remove from the heat, cover, and set aside.

Assembly. Bring the stock to a gentle simmer in a large stockpot. Gently reheat the Thyme-Lemon Jus and remove the bay leaf from the tomato fondue. Poach the lamb loins for about $3^{1/2}$ minutes, or until pink. Reserve the poaching stock for another use. Transfer the lamb loins to a cutting board and remove the strings. Slice the loins $^{1/2}$ inch thick. Arrange 5 slices of lamb, not overlapping, on each of 6 heated serving plates and place a generous mound of tomato fondue in the center. Spoon some of the jus around the edge of the plates and serve immediately.

Sautéed Mussels with Spicy Broth on Creamy Polenta

Yield: 6 servings

This dish could be served as a main course or a starter for eight, followed by a simple roast chicken or my Roasted Cornish Hens with Wilted Greens and Lentils (page 120). When broth and juices are combined with a starch such as polenta, as they are in this recipe, a new sort of sauce is created. This is not a dish for an elaborate dinner. It should be shared with friends who aren't shy about eating with their hands. Place the finished dish in the center of the table and invite everyone to dig in.

Polenta

2 cups water

1/2 teaspoon salt

1 1/2 cups polenta or coarsely ground yellow cornmeal

1 teaspoon togarashi seasonings (Japanese pepper), plus additional for garnish

1 cup heavy cream

1 tablespoon chopped mixed fresh herbs (such as parsley, oregano, chives)

Mussels

2 cups unsalted butter, cut into small pieces

4 cloves garlic, finely chopped

2 shallots, finely chopped

1 cup white wine

1 tablespoon sweet paprika

2 teaspoons togarashi seasonings

2 tablespoons finely chopped flat-leaf parsley

2 tablespoons finely chopped chives, plus additional for garnish

2 tablespoons finely chopped fresh rosemary

4 dozen mussels

Salt and freshly ground black pepper to taste

Polenta. In a heavy saucepan, combine the water and salt over medium-high heat. When the water is simmering, add polenta in a thin, steady stream, whisking continuously in the same direction until all the grains are absorbed and the mixture is smooth. Stir in the togarashi seasonings and cream. Decrease the heat to very low, switch to a wooden paddle, and stir continuously for about 10 minutes, or until the mixture is thickened and soft. Stir in the mixed herbs, cover, and set aside.

Mussels. In a large saucepan with a tight-fitting lid, heat 1/2 cup of the butter over medium-low heat. Add the garlic and shallots and sauté while stirring for 3 to 4 minutes, or until softened. Add the white wine, paprika, togarashi, and 1 tablespoon each parsley, chives, and rosemary. When the mixture is simmering, add the mussels, then cover the pan. Shake the pan every 2 minutes to redistribute and evenly cook the mussels. When the shells have opened (about 6 to 8 minutes), remove the pan from the heat and add the remaining 1 1/2 cups of butter, the remaining 1 tablespoon each of parsley, chives, and rosemary, and the salt and pepper. Shake the pan to help the butter become absorbed into the sauce.

Assembly. Spoon a large mound of the soft polenta into the center of 6 large heated bowls. Divide the mussels among the bowls, placing them around the perimeter of the polenta. Pour a generous amount of the cooking broth over each serving, scatter a few chives over the polenta, and dust the edges of the plates with the additional togarashi. Serve immediately.

Pan-Roasted Chicken Breasts on Curried Eggplant Purée with Polenta Fries and Lemon Chutney

Yield: 6 servings

When I teach cooking classes I often talk about the building blocks of fine cuisine.. This particular recipe contains several of them and, when combined, they make a quite extraordinary dish. This one in particular has become one of our most popular entrées. The curried eggplant can be used in many other dishes. The polenta fries and the lemon chutney are also versatile components that create a texture and flavor combination that really vibrates. The polenta needs to set overnight before it is cut into fries, so be sure to plan ahead. The chutney will keep in the refrigerator for 2 to 3 weeks and can also be served with barbecued grilled chicken or braised lamb shanks.

Lemon Chutney
1 cup golden raisins
1 cup raisins
Zest and juice of 2 lemons
2 yellow onions, finely chopped
1 teaspoon crushed red pepper flakes
1 cup plus 2 tablespoons apple cider vinegar
$1/3$ cup sugar

Polenta Fries
2 cups Chicken Stock (page 186)
2 cups heavy cream
1 teaspoon salt
$1/2$ teaspoon freshly ground white pepper
$1/2$ tablespoon unsalted butter
$1/2$ teaspoon ground nutmeg
2 cups polenta or coarsely ground yellow cornmeal
2 large eggs
1 cup grated Parmesan cheese

Eggplant Purée
3 large eggplants
2 tablespoons olive oil
1 tablespoon unsalted butter

1 small yellow onion, coarsely chopped
2 cloves garlic, finely chopped
$1 1/2$ tablespoons Madras-style curry powder
3 plum tomatoes, peeled, seeded, and cut into
  $1/4$-inch dice (page 202)
$1/2$ teaspoon salt
Freshly ground black pepper to taste
$1/4$ cup basil chiffonade (about 15 leaves)

Vegetable oil for deep-frying

Chicken
3 whole chicken breasts, halved, rib bones
  removed but wing joints still attached
Salt and freshly ground black pepper to taste
1 tablespoon vegetable oil

3 cups (about 3 ounces) frisée leaves
2 tablespoons Balsamic Vinaigrette (page 193)

Lemon Chutney. In a large nonreactive saucepan, combine all the ingredients. Bring to a simmer and cook partially covered for 30 to 35 minutes, or until almost all of the liquid has evaporated. Stir occasionally to keep all the ingredients evenly moistened. Cover and set aside.

Polenta. Line an 8 x 12-inch roasting pan with parchment paper and set aside. In a large, heavy saucepan, combine the stock and cream and bring to a boil, preventing the liquid from boiling over. Add the salt, white pepper, butter, and nutmeg and lower the heat. When the liquid is simmering, add the polenta in a thin, steady stream, whisking continuously in the same direction until all the grains are absorbed and the mixture is smooth. Decrease the heat to very low. Switch to a wooden paddle and stir the polenta continuously for 2 to 3 minutes, or until it begins to thicken. Add 1 egg, stirring until it is absorbed. Stir for 1 minute more, then stir in the remaining egg. Remove from the heat and stir in the Parmesan. The mixture will be very thick and pale yellow.

Mound the polenta mixture in the prepared roasting pan and, using a spatula repeatedly dipped into very hot water, spread the polenta into an even layer just less than $^1/_2$ inch thick. Cover with a kitchen towel and refrigerate for at least 6 hours or overnight.

Purée. Preheat the oven to 350°. Cut the eggplants in half lengthwise and brush them with the olive oil. Place cut side down on a baking sheet, and roast for about 45 minutes, or until very soft. Remove from the oven and, when cool enough to handle, scoop out the pulp and place it in a sieve lined with a double thickness of slightly dampened cheesecloth. Drain over a bowl for 1 hour. Bring the corners of the cheesecloth together and squeeze as much of the remaining moisture as possible from the pulp. In a food processor, purée the eggplant pulp until completely smooth, scraping down the sides of the bowl as necessary. Transfer to a large mixing bowl and set aside.

Heat a small skillet over medium-high heat and add the butter. Add the onion and garlic and sauté, stirring occasionally, for 3 to 4 minutes, or until softened. Add the curry powder and cook for 1 minute more. Add the tomatoes, stir to mix, and remove from the heat. Let the mixture cool for 5 minutes and then fold it into the puréed eggplant. Add the salt and pepper and set aside. Stir in the basil just before serving. (The purée can be made up to 4 hours in advance.)

Fries. In a large, heavy saucepan or deep-fryer, heat 4 to 5 inches of oil to 375°. Cut the polenta into twenty-four 4 x 3/4-inch batons. Deep-fry one-third of the batons for about 4 minutes each, or until deep golden brown outside but still pale yellow inside. Using a skimmer, transfer the fries to a paper towel–lined platter. Let the oil return to 375° before frying the second and third batches.

Chicken. Preheat the oven to 350°. Place a baking sheet in the oven to heat. Season the chicken breasts with salt and pepper. Heat a large, heavy skillet over medium-high heat and add the vegetable oil. Add the chicken breasts and sauté, skin side down, for about 4 minutes, or until golden brown (you may need to do this in 2 batches). Transfer the breasts to the baking sheet for 10 to 12 minutes more to finish cooking, or until cooked all the way through and no trace of pink remains.

Assembly. Turn off the oven and reheat the polenta fries in it as it cools. In a small bowl, toss the frisée with the vinaigrette until all the leaves are evenly coated.

Cut each chicken breast into 3 roughly triangular pieces. Stir the basil into the Eggplant Purée, then make a mound of the purée on one side of each of 6 serving plates. Place a mound of the frisée next to the purée. Set the pieces of chicken breast on top of the purée. Lean 4 polenta fries up against the purée and place a small dollop of chutney on the side. Serve immediately.

**BAKED GOODS
AND SWEETS**

Cherry-Cheese Streusel Coffee Cake

Yield: 20 servings

This lovely coffee cake would also make a terrific afternoon tea cake. Although it is somewhat complicated to make, you will love it if you like yeast-dough coffee cakes. (See photo on page 143.)

Streusel
1 cup cold unsalted butter, cut into 16 pieces
$1/2$ cup granulated sugar
$1^3/4$ cups all-purpose flour

Yeast Dough
$1/2$ ounce fresh yeast (page 81)
1 tablespoon warm water
$1/2$ cup water or milk plus 1 tablespoon,
   if necessary
$2^1/4$ cups bread flour
2 tablespoons unsalted butter, at
   room temperature
2 tablespoons granulated sugar
$1/2$ teaspoon salt

Cherry-Cheese Filling
2 cups sour cherries in syrup
$1^1/2$ tablespoons cornstarch
1 tablespoon water
$1/4$ teaspoon ground cinnamon
$1^1/2$ cups Quark Cheese (page 190)
Scant $1/2$ cup granulated sugar
1 tablespoon freshly squeezed lemon juice
$3/4$ teaspoon pure vanilla extract
5 large egg whites
Confectioners sugar, for dusting

Streusel. In a large, cold mixing bowl, combine all the ingredients and cut in the butter with a pastry blender or 2 knives until the mixture resembles fine, moist bread crumbs. Bring the mixture together and compact it into a firm ball, then press it through the $1/4$-inch square holes of a cooling rack. The streusel mixture should look something like small croutons or large, coarse bread crumbs. Cover and chill until needed.

Dough. In a small bowl, whisk the yeast and the warm water with a fork until smooth, then set aside. In the bowl of a heavy-duty electric mixer fitted with the dough hook, combine the milk, bread flour, butter, sugar, and salt and blend at slow speed for 2 minutes, scraping down the sides of the bowl as necessary. If the dough is crumbly and does not come together in $1^1/2$ to 2 minutes, add the extra tablespoon of water or milk. Add the yeast mixture and continue to mix until the dough is firm and smooth, about 6 minutes more. Turn the dough out onto a lightly floured surface and bring together into a ball, then allow to rest, covered with a cloth, for 10 minutes while you make the filling.

Filling. Place the cherries and their syrup in a medium saucepan and set over medium-low heat until hot. In a small bowl, combine the cornstarch and water and stir together until smooth. Add the cinnamon and stir the mixture into the cherries. Continue cooking and stirring until the mixture is hot and very thick. Remove from the heat and let cool to room temperature. In a medium mixing bowl, combine the cheese, sugar, lemon juice, and vanilla and stir until smooth. In a separate bowl, beat the egg whites to stiff peaks. Fold the egg whites into the cheese mixture. Fold the cheese mixture into the cherries.

Assembly. Preheat the oven to 375°. Lightly oil an 18 x 13-inch baking sheet with 2-inch-high sides.

On a lightly floured surface, roll the pastry out into a 14 x 19-inch rectangle. Transfer the pastry to the prepared baking sheet, pressing it into the corners and about $1^1/_2$ inches up the sides. Pour the filling into the pastry shell and spread it evenly, then let rise in a very warm, moist place until the outer edges of the dough are puffy and dimpled, about 30 minutes. Distribute the streusel mixture evenly over the top and bake the cake for 10 minutes. Reduce the temperature to 325° and bake for 10 to 20 minutes more, or until the edges of the pastry are golden and the filling is set. Cool on a rack. When warm, dust with the confectioners sugar and cut into squares. Serve warm or at room temperature.

Hazelnut Streusel Coffee Cake

Yield: 10 to 12 servings

Although this is quite an involved recipe, everything can be made ahead of time and assembled just before you plan to bake the coffee cake. Or, it can be baked in advance and kept in an airtight container for at least 3 days before serving. Since the dough is fairly firm, make sure the bowl of your electric mixer is firmly seated before you begin to mix. If desired, drizzle the warm coffee cake with a simple icing after you've brushed it with the apricot preserves. When you slice into the braided cake and see all the layers, you will be thrilled and amazed. (See photo on page 143.)

Streusel

1 cup cold unsalted butter, cut into 16 pieces

$^1/_2$ cup sugar

$1^3/_4$ cups all-purpose flour

Filling

$1^1/_4$ cups coarsely chopped toasted hazelnuts (page 203)

$^3/_4$ ounce Nougat (page 200)

2 tablespoons dry bread crumbs

$^1/_4$ teaspoon unsweetened cocoa powder

$^1/_4$ teaspoon light rum

$^2/_3$ cup milk

$^1/_2$ cup sugar

Yeast Dough

$^1/_2$ ounce fresh yeast (page 81)

1 tablespoon warm water

$^1/_2$ cup water or milk plus 1 tablespoon, if necessary

$2^1/_4$ cups bread flour

2 tablespoons unsalted butter, at room temperature

2 tablespoons sugar

$^1/_2$ teaspoon salt

$^3/_4$ cup warmed apricot preserves, optional

Streusel. In a large, chilled mixing bowl, combine all the ingredients and cut in the butter with a pastry blender or 2 knives until the mixture resembles fine, moist bread crumbs. Bring the mixture together and compact it into a firm ball, then press it through the $^1/_4$-inch square holes of a cooling rack. The streusel mixture should look something like small croutons or large, coarse bread crumbs. Cover and chill until needed.

Filling. In a medium mixing bowl, combine the hazelnuts, nougat, bread crumbs, cocoa powder, and rum and toss together until evenly blended. In a small saucepan, combine the milk and sugar over medium heat. Stir together until the milk is very hot and the sugar has dissolved, but do not let it boil. Stir the hot milk into the dry ingredients, mixing until evenly blended, then allow to cool before using.

Dough. In a small bowl, whisk the yeast and warm water with a fork until smooth, then set aside. In the bowl of a heavy-duty electric mixer fitted with the dough hook, combine the milk, flour, butter, sugar, and salt and blend at slow speed for 2 minutes, scraping down the sides of the bowl as necessary. If the dough is crumbly and does not come together in 1½ to 2 minutes, add the extra tablespoon of milk. Add the yeast mixture and continue to mix until the dough is firm and smooth, about 6 minutes more. Turn the dough out onto a lightly floured surface and bring together into a ball. Cover with a kitchen towel and let rest for 5 minutes.

Assembly. Line a large baking sheet with parchment paper. On a lightly floured work surface, roll the dough out into an 11 x 15-inch rectangle. Spread the hazelnut filling evenly over it with a flexible pastry scraper. Starting at one of the short ends, roll up the dough into a tight cylinder, then cut it in half lengthwise with a serrated knife. Twist the dough into a very thick braid with the cut sides facing upward, and transfer it to the prepared baking sheet.

Gently mound and press the streusel over the coffee cake. Set the cake to rise in a warm, moist place until it is about 1½ times its original size, about 30 to 50 minutes.

Preheat the oven to 400°. Place a cast-iron skillet on the bottom oven rack to heat. When the skillet is hot, open the oven door, pour a cup of cold water into the pan, and place the coffee cake on the center oven rack. Bake for 10 minutes, then lower the oven temperature to 325° and remove the cast iron pan. Bake for 45 to 50 minutes more, or until the pastry is firm and brown and a long skewer comes out clean when inserted in the center. Remove from the oven and brush with the warm apricot preserves. Let cool slightly, then serve. The coffee cake keeps in an airtight container for at least 3 days.

Walnut Sourdough Bread

Yield: 2 large round loaves

Get some sourdough starter from a friendly neighborhood bakery, or make your own following the directions in one of the many available bread books. This bread dough must be made by hand because the walnuts would be broken up by the action of the dough hook. (See photo on page 143.)

2½ cups warm water

1 cup sourdough starter

1½ cups whole-wheat flour

2 tablespoons olive oil

1 tablespoon sugar

½ tablespoon salt

½ ounce fresh yeast (page 81)

2 tablespoons warm water

2 cups bread flour

¾ cup walnut halves

Warm a large metal mixing bowl with hot water, then pour it out and wipe the bowl dry. Combine the warm water and sourdough starter in the bowl and stir to mix. Leave the mixture (the "sponge") at very warm room temperature (up to 85°) until it is puffed and slightly bubbly, about 30 minutes.

With a wooden spoon, stir in the whole-wheat flour, olive oil, sugar, and salt and mix until evenly blended. The dough will be sticky and very loose.

In a small bowl, whisk the yeast and the warm water until smooth. Add the yeast mixture, the bread flour, and the walnut halves to the sponge and mix in with one hand, using a scooping and turning action to evenly blend the dough, which will still be very loose and sticky. Sprinkle a little more whole-wheat flour over the top of the sponge, then cover the bowl tightly with plastic wrap. Let the sponge rise overnight in the refrigerator, making sure it has plenty of headroom as it will get quite large.

The next morning, line a large baking sheet with parchment paper and generously flour the work surface. Turn the dough out onto the work surface and knead, adding a little more flour if necessary, until it is smooth but soft. Shape the dough into 2 large rounds, about 23 ounces each.

Preheat the oven to 400°. Transfer the loaves to the prepared baking sheet and set them in a warm, moist place to rise for 30 to 50 minutes, depending on the temperature, or until they are puffy and about one and a half times their original size. Bake the loaves for 15 minutes, then reduce the heat to 350° and continue cooking for 40 to 50 minutes, or until the bottom of each loaf makes a hollow sound when tapped. Slice while slightly warm or cool and serve. The bread will keep, tightly wrapped, for 5 days.

English Muffin Bread

Yield: 2 large loaves

*This bread is beautiful for sandwiches and toast.
Don't overwork the dough or add too much flour;
the dough must be light for the bread to rise well
enough to have big holes.*

1 ounce fresh yeast (page 81)
2½ tablespoons sugar
2 tablespoons warm water
4½ cups all-purpose flour
2 teaspoons salt
2 teaspoons baking soda
2 cups warm milk

In a small bowl, stir together the yeast and sugar.
Add the warm water and whisk until smooth.

In the bowl of a heavy-duty electric mixer fitted
with the dough hook, combine the flour, salt,
and baking soda and mix together. With the
mixer on low, gradually add the milk, then mix
for 1 minute more, scraping down the bowl and
the dough hook as necessary. Add the yeast
mixture and continue to mix for about 10 minutes, scraping down the bowl and hook as necessary, until you have a stiff, glossy, elastic dough.
(If the mixture is too firm for your electric mixer
to handle, finish kneading it by hand.)

Turn the dough out onto a lightly floured surface
and cut in half. With the palm of your hand,
work the air out of each piece of dough and,
cupping it in your hands, work it back and forth
into a smooth ball. Repeat with the other piece
of dough. Cover both rounds with a towel and let
rest for 10 minutes. Sprinkle a little flour over the
top of the rounds, then roll them out to approximately ½ inch thick. Starting with a long side,
tightly roll up the dough to form a long cylinder.
Pinch the ends together firmly, then tuck them
under. Repeat with the other piece of dough.

Preheat the oven to 375°. Lightly oil two 10 x 4-
inch loaf pans. Drop the loaves into the prepared
pans and place them in a warm, moist place to
rise until doubled in size, about 30 to 50 minutes. Bake for 30 to 35 minutes, or until the tops
are golden and the bottoms sound hollow when
tapped. Cool on a rack. Slice ½ to ¾ inch thick
and use as directed or as sandwich bread. The
bread keeps, tightly wrapped, for 3 or 4 days.

Pretzel Dough

Yield: 10 pretzels, 8 pretzel rolls or pretzel buns, or 2 loaves pretzel bread

I love all kinds of pretzels, and I make them in every shape imaginable. We have tested this recipe exhaustively and found it works really well in a home kitchen. In fact, I think the recipe is so good it's going to make us famous! You can make these in any shape and flavor you want (I'm partial to cheese pretzels).

A note of warning: This is a very stiff dough. It could tire your mixer if you don't watch carefully and hold the mixer steady as it works.

1 ounce fresh yeast (page 81)
1¼ cups warm water
3¾ cups bread flour
2 teaspoons salt
¼ cup unsalted butter, softened
3 tablespoons baking soda
2 quarts water
1 large egg yolk, lightly beaten
    with 2 teaspoons water
Coarse salt to taste

In a small bowl, whisk the yeast and ¼ cup of the water until smooth.

In the bowl of a heavy-duty electric mixer fitted with the dough hook, combine the remaining 1 cup water, the bread flour, yeast mixture, salt, and butter. Mix at slow speed for 3 minutes, scraping down the sides of the bowl and the hook as necessary to make sure the mixture blends evenly. When the ingredients are well combined, increase the mixer speed to high and continue mixing and occasionally scraping for about 8 minutes more, or until the dough is firm and elastic. (If the mixture is too firm for the mixer to handle, finish kneading it by hand.) Turn the ball of dough out onto a lightly floured work surface and let rest for 5 minutes, loosely covered with a kitchen towel. Line a baking sheet that will fit in your freezer with parchment paper and set aside. Shape as follows, depending on which form you wish to make. (Do not add more flour to the work surface unless absolutely necessary; the dough should be a little sticky.)

Pretzels (requires 2 prepared baking sheets): Cut the dough into 10 pieces approximately 3 ounces in size. Roll each into a 5-inch-long cylinder about 1 inch in diameter. With the palms of your hands, roll each ball into a long rope (about 2 feet) with the ends much thinner than the center portion. Twist the two ends together twice about 4 inches in from the ends. Fold the rope, pressing the little tips onto the larger central part of the rope about 3 inches apart (see below). Place on the prepared baking sheet. Repeat with the remaining ropes.

continued

Hazelnut Streusel Coffee Cake (left back), Walnut Sourdough Bread (center), Pretzel Buns (right back), Pretzels
(right front), Pretzel Rolls (left center), and Cherry–
Cheese Streusel Coffee Cake (left front)

Pretzel Dough *continued*

Pretzel Rolls (requires 2 prepared baking sheets): Cut the dough into 8 equal pieces approximately 4 ounces in size. Roll each into a 5-inch-long cylinder about 1 inch in diameter. With the palms of your hands, roll each cylinder into a rope about 12 inches long, of even thickness throughout the entire length. Tie the rope into a loose knot in the center, then tuck the ends under the middle and mold gently into an attractive shape. Place on the prepared baking sheet. Repeat with the remaining pieces of dough.

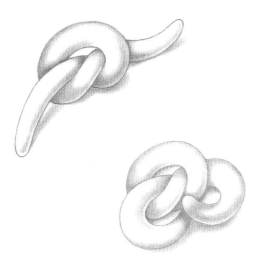

Pretzel Buns: Cut the dough into 8 pieces approximately 4 ounces in size. With your hands slightly cupped, roll and mold the pieces with your palms into round, tall balls of dough. Place on the prepared baking sheet.

Pretzel Bread: Cut the dough into 2 equal pieces. Roll each piece into a long, fat, cylindrical loaf, then tuck the ends under. Place the loaves on the prepared baking sheet.

When the pretzel dough is shaped, let it sit in a very warm, moist place to rise until almost doubled in size, about 30 to 50 minutes.

Freeze the shaped, risen pretzel dough, uncovered, on the baking sheet(s) for at least 2 hours and up to 24 hours; the dough should be frozen solid.

Before removing the pretzels from the freezer, combine the baking soda and water in a large saucepan and bring it to a simmer. Preheat the oven to 425°. Remove the pan from the freezer and, using a large, flat skimmer, dip each frozen pretzel, roll, bun, or loaf of bread in the simmering water for about 3 seconds, letting the excess water drain before returning it to the baking sheet. Brush the pretzels with the egg yolk–water mixture, then sprinkle coarse salt over them. Immediately place the baking sheet in the hot oven. Bake all the different pretzel shapes for 10 minutes, then lower the oven temperature to 375° and bake the pretzels for 5 to 8 minutes more, the buns and rolls for 8 to 12 minutes more, and the bread for 20 to 25 minutes more.

Once cool, the pretzels keep in an airtight container for 1 day. After that, use them to make Pretzel Knödel (page 182).

Focaccia Bread

Yield: One 13 x 9-inch focaccia

This is a very simple white focaccia made without a starter. It is perfect for the sandwiches in this book. If you decide to use active dry yeast to make this dough, make sure the water is hotter than for fresh yeast, between 110° and 115° (for more about this, see page 81).

▶ 1 ounce fresh yeast or 2 packages (5 teaspoons) active dry yeast (page 81)
2 teaspoons sugar
1 1/2 cups warm water
3 cups unbleached all-purpose flour
2 tablespoons salt
1/3 cup olive oil
1 teaspoon coarse sea salt

In a small bowl, stir the yeast, sugar, and 1/2 cup of the warm water with a fork until smooth. Let the mixture proof 10 minutes, or until it is bubbly.

In the bowl of a heavy-duty electric mixer fitted with the flat beater, combine the flour, salt, remaining 1 cup warm water, and olive oil and mix at low speed for 2 minutes. Add the yeast mixture, switch to the dough hook attachment, and continue to mix until the dough is firm and smooth, about 6 minutes.

Turn the dough out onto a lightly floured surface and bring together into a firm, round ball. Lightly oil a large mixing bowl, place the dough in it, and turn to coat lightly with oil. Cover the bowl with plastic wrap and let rise in a warm place for 1 to 1 1/2 hours, or until doubled in bulk.

Oil a 13 x 9-inch rimmed baking sheet and roll the dough out to a rectangle just smaller than the pan size. Cover the dough with a damp towel and let it rest for 5 minutes to relax the stretchy and resistant glutens.

Preheat the oven to 450°. Transfer the dough to the baking sheet and press it evenly into the edges and corners with your fingertips. Again, cover with the damp towel and let rise in a warm place for 45 minutes, or until risen, puffy, and full of air holes.

With your knuckles, press dimples into the top of the dough about 2 inches apart and then brush with olive oil. Sprinkle the sea salt evenly over the top and bake for about 15 minutes, or until the bottom of the crust is golden and the focaccia sounds hollow when tapped with a knuckle.

Remove the focaccia from the pan immediately and transfer it to a rack to cool so it does not become soggy. Serve warm, or cool to room temperature and slice as needed.

Decorated Bread Roll Rings

Yield: 3 bread roll rings or 18 rolls

These pretty bread roll rings are perfect for dinner parties of up to 6 people. They are made to be shared with friends—when you break them apart and separate all the different rolls from the ring, it's a real attention-grabber. You can make the toppings as interesting or as plain as you like. You can also mix the flavorings into the dough instead of sprinkling them on top. Just divide up the dough and mix a different flavoring into each. Be careful not to put too much cheese on top or it will run off and stick to your baking sheet!

▶ Rolls

1 ounce fresh yeast (page 81)

1^1/$_2$ cups warm water

3^1/$_2$ cups bread flour

1^1/$_2$ tablespoons rye flour

1 tablespoon salt

Toppings (choose 6 of the following)

2 tablespoons sweet paprika

2 tablespoons crushed pepper flakes

^{1}/$_4$ cup coarsely grated Swiss cheese

2 tablespoons poppy seeds

2 tablespoons sesame seeds

2 tablespoons rolled oats

2 tablespoons mixed seeds (such as flax, sesame, sunflower)

^{1}/$_4$ cup coarsely chopped kalamata olives

4 dry-packed sundried tomatoes or Home-Cured Tomatoes (page 186), soaked in boiling water for 20 minutes, drained, and coarsely chopped

In a small bowl, whisk the yeast with ^{1}/$_2$ cup of the warm water until smooth.

In the bowl of a heavy-duty electric mixer fitted with the dough hook, combine the remaining 2 cups of warm water with the bread flour, rye flour, and salt. Mix at low speed, scraping the sides of the bowl and the hook as necessary, for 3 minutes. Add the yeast mixture and continue mixing at low speed for 5 minutes more. Increase the mixer speed to high and mix until you have a firm, dry dough. Turn out onto a lightly floured surface, cover with a kitchen towel, and let rest for 5 minutes.

Lightly oil 2 large baking sheets. Divide the dough into approximately 2-ounce pieces. With your hand cupped over a piece of dough, roll it into a round, firm ball about the size of a tangerine. Repeat until you have shaped all the pieces. Place 6 of the balls ^{1}/$_2$ inch away from each other in a circle on a baking sheet, and repeat with the other balls to form 3 bread roll rings. Alternatively, make individual rolls, placing them at least 1 inch apart on the baking sheet. Using a spray bottle, spritz the balls of dough with water.

Sprinkle a tiny bit of each of 6 toppings on the rolls, so that every roll in the rings has a different topping, and repeat with the other bread rings. Let rise in a very warm, moist place until the rolls have risen to about 1^1/$_2$ times their original size and are touching each other.

Preheat the oven to 400°. Bake the rolls for 10 to 15 minutes, or until they are risen and golden, and sound hollow when tapped on the bottom. Serve immediately.

Lebküchen (Honey and Spice Cookies)

Yield: 24 cookies

This is a traditional German gingerbread cookie that can be glazed or unglazed, or covered with chocolate, depending on your whim. The city of Nüremberg is famous for its lebküchen, and Nüremberger lebküchen are truly fantastic. If you can find the obladen wafers and the lebküchen spices (look for them at specialty markets that stock imported European foods), try this cookie. I guarantee you'll be serving it at Christmas for the rest of your life.

▶ Lebküchen

24 obladen or thin wafers

4 large eggs

³/₄ cup plus 2 tablespoons granulated sugar

2 tablespoons vanilla sugar (see Note)

2¹/₂ ounces finely chopped candied lemon zest

Zest of 1 lemon

1 lemon, peel and pith removed, coarsely chopped

1 teaspoon lebküchen spices

³/₄ cup plus 2 tablespoons finely ground blanched almonds (almond meal)

³/₄ cup plus 2 tablespoons finely ground toasted hazelnuts (page 203)

1³/₄ cups all-purpose flour

1 teaspoon baking powder

Glaze

1 large egg white

2 teaspoons light rum

2 cups confectioners sugar

1 teaspoon melted butter

Candy balls, glitter, or other fancy patisserie decorations, optional

Lebküchen. Line 2 large baking sheets with parchment paper and place 12 obladen wafers on each one. Set aside.

Preheat the oven to 350°. In a very large mixing bowl, combine the eggs and granulated and vanilla sugars and beat until the mixture is pale yellow and will hold a ribbon when the beater is lifted away. In a separate bowl, combine the candied and fresh lemon zests, lemon flesh, lebküchen spices, and ground nuts. Sift the flour and the baking powder over the zest mixture and mix thoroughly. Fold the flour and zest mixture into the eggs until evenly mixed, then spread about 3 tablespoons of the mixture on each wafer.

Bake the lebküchen for about 20 minutes, or until light brown. Transfer the cookies to cooling racks and immediately make the glaze.

Glaze. Beat together the egg white, rum, and confectioners sugar until a thick paste forms, then drizzle in the butter. If necessary, add a little more rum or a dash of lemon juice and combine well to make a very thick syrup (it should be thick enough to stick to the cookies as you glaze them). Using a pastry brush, paint the glaze evenly over the tops of the warm cookies and sprinkle with the decorative candy.

Note: Vanilla sugar is available at specialty gourmet stores, but it's more economical to make your own. The next time you split a vanilla pod to scrape out the seeds, wash and thoroughly dry the pod, then add it to 1 pound of granulated sugar. Tightly cover the vanilla sugar and store until needed.

Röckenwagner's Triple-Fudge Brownies

Yield: 8 to 10 brownies

*I prefer to add 1 cup of coarsely chopped walnuts
to this recipe, but the brownies are just as addictive
without them. These are not light and fluffy brownies. They're very rich—almost like candy—so you
don't need to cut them very big. They will keep in an
airtight container for 1 week.*

½ cup unsalted butter

1½ cups semisweet chocolate chips

1 ounce unsweetened chocolate, broken
   into chunks

½ ounce bittersweet chocolate, broken in half

2 large eggs

1 large egg yolk

2 teaspoons powdered instant espresso

½ tablespoon pure vanilla extract

½ cup sugar

¼ cup all-purpose flour

¾ teaspoon baking powder

¼ teaspoon salt

1 cup walnut pieces, lightly toasted (page 203)

Butter and flour a 13 x 9-inch baking pan with
2-inch sides. Set aside.

In the top of a double boiler over barely simmering water, combine the butter, ³/4 cup of the
chocolate chips, the unsweetened chocolate,
and the bittersweet chocolate. Stir occasionally
until melted and smooth. Remove from the heat
and stir occasionally until the mixture cools to
room temperature.

Preheat the oven to 400°.

In a large mixing bowl, combine the eggs,
egg yolk, espresso powder, vanilla, and sugar.
Beat together until the mixture will hold a
ribbon when the beater is lifted away. Add the
cooled chocolate mixture and stir only until
just combined.

Sift the flour, baking powder, and salt together.
Sprinkle half over the chocolate mixture and
mix well with a wooden spoon. Repeat with the
remaining flour mixture. The batter will be very
thick. Finally, stir in the remaining ³/4 cup
chocolate chips and the walnuts. Pour the batter
into the prepared pan and smooth out evenly.
Bake for 15 minutes, or until firm in the center.
Do not overbake; the center should be quite
moist, almost gooey when tested with a toothpick. Let cool completely in the pan on a rack
before cutting into squares.

Espresso-Macadamia Nut Cookies

Yield: 20 to 25 cookies

This cookie is very similar to the Röckenwagner Triple-Fudge Brownies, but the macadamia nuts make it special. You will want to use whole macadamias rather than chopping them—the crunch of the whole nuts in the soft cookies is tremendous.

4 ounces unsweetened chocolate,
   coarsely chopped

3 cups semisweet chocolate chips

¹/₂ cup unsalted butter

¹/₂ cup all-purpose flour

¹/₂ teaspoon baking powder

¹/₂ teaspoon salt

4 large eggs

1¹/₂ cups sugar

1¹/₂ tablespoons instant espresso powder

2 teaspoons pure vanilla extract

50 whole macadamia nuts

In the top of a double boiler over gently simmering water, melt the unsweetened chocolate, 1¹/₂ cups of the chocolate chips, and the butter, stirring occasionally until the mixture is smooth and completely blended. Set aside to cool to room temperature.

In a medium mixing bowl, sift together the flour, baking powder, and salt and set aside. In a large mixing bowl, combine the eggs, sugar, espresso powder, and vanilla and beat together until the mixture holds a ribbon when the beater is lifted away. Fold in the cooled chocolate mixture, sift half of the flour mixture over the top and fold it in gently. Repeat with the remaining flour mixture. Fold in the remaining chocolate chips and the macadamia nuts. Let the batter rest for 30 minutes, covered, in the refrigerator.

Preheat the oven to 400°. Butter and flour 2 large baking sheets. Spoon about 2 tablespoons of cookie batter at a time onto the prepared baking sheet, placing the cookies at least 1 inch apart and making sure the nuts are evenly distributed. Bake for 7 to 10 minutes, or until puffy and shiny. Cool on a rack. Serve warm or at room temperature.

Fruit Tart with Streusel Topping

Yield: one 11-inch tart

This is my master recipe for a very versatile tart. I have given three fruit variations here, but you could also make the tart with peaches, apricots, pears— almost any soft fruit. The dough is the same, and the egg-cream mixture, which is called a "royale," is almost the same for each variation. With some fruits, you might want to add a little extra flavoring to the royale (such as the cinnamon in the plum tart.) The tarts are best at room temperature, but they are also good when still warm from the oven.

Streusel Topping

1¼ cups all-purpose flour

½ cup cold unsalted butter, cut into ¼-inch pieces

½ cup sugar

½ teaspoon pure vanilla extract

Dough

1¾ cups all-purpose flour

Scant ½ cup sugar

¼ teaspoon salt

½ teaspoon baking powder

½ cup unsalted butter, cut into small pieces

1 large egg, lightly beaten

2 tablespoons cold water

½ teaspoon pure vanilla extract

Apple Filling

4 apples (about 1¼ pounds), peeled, cored, and cut into ¼-inch slivers

3 large eggs

¼ cup sugar

1 teaspoon pure vanilla extract

¼ cup heavy cream

Streusel. In a large bowl, combine all the ingredients. Rub the mixture together between the palms of your hands until it is well blended and resembles large peas. Set aside. (The streusel topping can be covered and refrigerated for up to 5 days.)

Dough. In the bowl of a food processor, combine the flour, sugar, salt, and baking powder. Pulse until evenly blended. Add the butter and process in short bursts until the mixture resembles coarse bread crumbs. Add the egg, 1 tablespoon of the cold water, and the vanilla and pulse just until the dough clumps. Add part or all of the remaining tablespoon of water only if the dough does not form a clump within the first 5 or 10 seconds. The dough should be fairly dry. Turn the dough out onto a lightly floured surface and quickly work it into a ball. Cover with plastic wrap and refrigerate for 1 hour.

Butter and flour an 11-inch fluted tart pan with a removable bottom. Roll the dough out to ¼ inch thick and gently ease it into the prepared pan, pressing it into the corners and building up the sides. Prick the bottom of the shell with a fork and chill for 20 minutes. Preheat the oven to 350°.

Filling. Distribute the apple slivers evenly over the base of the tart. Place the tart in the oven for 5 minutes to dry the fruit slightly. Meanwhile, in a large bowl, whisk the eggs, sugar, vanilla, and cream until frothy and evenly blended. Alternatively, prepare the filling of your choice and proceed as directed (recipes follow). Remove the tart from the oven. Pour the egg mixture through a strainer into the tart shell and return the tart to the oven. After 4 minutes, or as soon as the filling has formed a skin and begun to set, sprinkle the streusel topping over the tart. Bake for 11 to 16 minutes, or until the filling is set and does not jiggle in the center. Cool on a rack. Serve at room temperature or cover and refrigerate for up to 1 day, return to room temperature, then serve.

Rhubarb Tart Filling

1¹/₂ **pounds fresh rhubarb, peeled and cut into ¹/₄-inch cubes**

³/₄ **cup sugar**

2 **tablespoons coarse yellow cornmeal**

3 **large eggs**

¹/₂ **teaspoon pure vanilla extract**

¹/₄ **cup heavy cream**

In a large nonreactive mixing bowl, combine the rhubarb and ¹/₂ cup of the sugar. Toss well and let sit at room temperature for 1 hour, then drain in a colander.

Sprinkle the cornmeal evenly over the base of the tart. Mound the drained rhubarb evenly in the tart shell and place in the preheated oven for 5 minutes to dry the fruit slightly. Meanwhile, in a large bowl, whisk the eggs, remaining ¹/₄ cup sugar, the vanilla, and cream until frothy and evenly blended. Remove the tart from the oven and proceed as directed.

Plum Tart Filling

2 **tablespoons mixed coarse dry bread crumbs**

1¹/₂ **pounds ripe plums, pitted and sliced ¹/₈ inch thick**

1 **teaspoon ground cinnamon**

3 **large eggs**

¹/₄ **cup sugar**

1 **teaspoon pure vanilla extract**

¹/₄ **cup heavy cream**

Sprinkle the bread crumbs evenly over the bottom of the tart shell. Distribute the plum slices evenly over the base of the tart, either in an abstract design or in concentric circles. Sprinkle the cinnamon over the fruit. Place the tart in the oven for 3 minutes to dry the fruit slightly. Meanwhile, in a large bowl, whisk the eggs, sugar, vanilla, and cream until frothy and evenly blended. Remove the tart from the oven and proceed as directed.

Raspberry Squares

Yield: twenty 3 x 3-inch squares

Be sure to use an excellent raspberry jam in these squares. The squares will stay fresh for about 2 days, but it's unlikely they'll stick around that long.

Raspberry Topping
2 cups raspberry jam
¹/₃ cup sugar

Dough
3 cups all-purpose flour
1 cup sugar
¹/₂ cup blanched sliced almonds, coarsely chopped
1¹/₄ cups unsalted butter, cut into 20 pieces
1 large egg, lightly beaten
¹/₃ to ¹/₂ cup cold water

1 large egg
2 teaspoons water
2 tablespoons sugar

Topping. In a small saucepan, combine the jam and the sugar over medium-low heat and whisk together until the sugar has melted and the jam is thinned and spreadable. Butter a 17 x 13-inch baking sheet with 2-inch-high sides. Preheat the oven to 400°.

Dough. In a large mixing bowl, combine the flour, sugar, and almonds and toss with your hands to mix evenly. Add the butter and blend by rubbing the mixture between your fingertips until it's the consistency of coarse, moist bread crumbs. Drizzle the egg evenly over the mixture and continue blending with your fingertips until the mixture is evenly moistened. Add ¹/₃ cup of water and blend just until the dough comes together into a ball, using 1 to 2 additional tablespoons of water, if necessary, to make a soft but not sticky dough.

Transfer the dough to a generously floured work surface and bring it together into a smooth ball. Wrap the dough in plastic wrap and refrigerate for 20 minutes. Cut the dough into 2 pieces, one slightly larger than the other. Sprinkle the larger piece of dough with a little flour and roll it out to a 17 x 13-inch rectangle. The dough is very delicate and will tear easily, but can also be easily patched. Be sure to keep the work surface well dusted with flour as you roll. When the dough is large enough, fold it over the rolling pin and transfer it to the pan, gently fitting it into the pan, then building up the edges and patching any holes and tears with your fingers.

Spread an even layer of raspberry topping over the bottom layer of dough. Roll out the remaining piece of dough to a 16 x 12-inch rectangle. Drape it over the rolling pin and transfer it to the pan, matching the edges as closely as possible. Gently press the edge of the pastry top against the sides of the tart to seal.

Gently whisk the egg and water together. Brush the top of the pastry with the egg mixture, then sprinkle evenly with the sugar.

Bake for 10 minutes, then lower the oven temperature to 350° and bake for 15 to 20 minutes more, or until the top is slightly golden and the pastry is firm. Remove from the oven and loosen the pastry by running a sharp knife along the inner rim of the pan (the pastry will shrink a little as it cools and may crack if it is not loosened). Cool in the pan on a rack and then cut into squares. The squares can be kept in an airtight container, separated by sheets of waxed paper, for at least 3 days.

Upside-Down Plum Tart

Yield: 8 to 10 servings

I prefer to make this dish as ten small cakes because I love being able to serve individual desserts. Of course, this works well at the restaurant, but it might not be ideal for the home cook, so I've included instructions for making one large cake.

Plum Sauce
8 ripe plums, pitted and quartered
1/3 cup water
1/3 cup sugar
1/2 stick cinnamon
2 teaspoons freshly squeezed lemon juice

Cake
4 tablespoons unsalted butter, at room temperature
1 cup granulated sugar
1 1/2 cups all-purpose flour
2 teaspoons baking powder
1 teaspoon ground cinnamon
1/4 teaspoon salt
1/2 cup milk
1 teaspoon pure vanilla extract
2 large eggs
1/2 cup unsalted butter
1 cup firmly packed brown sugar
6 plums, pitted and sliced about 3/8 inch thick

1 quart best-quality vanilla ice cream, optional

Sauce. Combine all the ingredients in a large nonreactive saucepan. Over medium-low heat, stir until the sugar has dissolved, then increase the heat to medium and partially cover. Stirring frequently, simmer the mixture for about 20 minutes, or until thickened. Transfer to a blender and blend for 30 seconds, scraping down the container as necessary. Push the mixture through a strainer into a bowl, pressing firmly on the solids and scraping the strainer to extract as much liquid as possible. Discard the solids. Set aside until ready to serve.

Cake. Preheat the oven to 350°. In the bowl of a heavy-duty electric mixer, cream the butter and sugar until pale and fluffy. In a separate bowl, combine the flour, baking powder, cinnamon, and salt. Sift one-third of the dry ingredients over the creamed mixture and beat until combined. Add about one-third of the milk and the vanilla, beat again, and continue adding the dry ingredients and milk, alternating, until all have been mixed in. Add the eggs one at a time, incorporating the first before adding the second.

In a small saucepan, melt the butter over medium-low heat, then add the brown sugar, and stir until the sugar has dissolved. Remove from the heat and pour the butter-sugar mixture into a 10-inch nonstick cake pan or divide among ten 3-inch nonstick tartlet pans. Arrange the sliced plums in concentric circles, alternating the direction of each ring, on the bottom of the pan. Pour the cake batter over the plums.

Bake the large cake for 30 minutes, the small cakes 18 to 20 minutes, or until the cake is firm and a toothpick comes out clean when inserted in the center. Cool on a rack for 10 minutes.

Run a sharp knife around the inside of the cake pan or tartlet pans to loosen the cake. Invert the cake(s) on a large serving platter or individual dessert plates. Spoon some of the sauce around the edges and serve immediately, with vanilla ice cream.

Fruit Soup with Berries, Sorbet, and Champagne

Yield: 4 servings

This soup uses prepared smoothie-type juice, which you can get almost anywhere now, including juice bars, health food stores, and good supermarkets. The smoothie adds texture and flavor to the dish, so do use it if you can. If you can't get the prepared smoothie, cut 1 banana into chunks and blend with ½ cup apple juice in a blender until smooth. The champagne contributes sparkle and a certain panache. This is a great summer dessert which has absolutely no fat!

1 cup pineapple juice

1 cup banana smoothie juice

½ cup orange juice

Juice of 1½ limes

1 apple, peeled

1 star anise

2 cups mixed berries (such as blueberries, raspberries, blackberries, gooseberries, and small strawberries)

4 scoops best-quality lemon sorbet

½ cup Champagne or sparkling wine

1 tablespoon basil chiffonade (about 4 leaves)

In a medium saucepan, combine the pineapple juice, banana smoothie, and orange and lime juices. Using the small end of a melon baller, cut as many rounds as possible from the apple, avoiding the core (you should have about ¾ cup). Add the star anise to the juices and, over medium heat, bring the mixture to a gentle simmer. Add the apple balls to the liquid and simmer until tender, about 10 minutes. Remove the pan from the heat and discard the star anise. Pour the mixture into a medium metal bowl and chill as quickly as possible. (You can hurry the process by nesting the bowl in a larger bowl filled with ice and water, and stirring occasionally.)

Gently stir the berries into the cold soup. Divide the soup among 4 chilled dessert bowls. Place a scoop of lemon sorbet in the center of each bowl and splash about 2 tablespoons of Champagne over the top. Sprinkle a pinch of the basil over each and serve immediately.

Macaronnade de Chocolate

Yield: 6 servings

Although I refer to it as a soufflé in the directions, that's not entirely accurate. It's not a soufflé, but it's not a cake either—it's somewhere in the middle. It's a little like the chocolate tartlets (page 160), but not as dense.

As I look through the dessert recipes I have included in the book, I am struck by something: for a guy who didn't used to like making chocolate desserts, I sure make a lot of them. Perhaps that's because I think people judge a restaurant by its chocolate desserts and Caesar salad. Once upon a time, I never would have thought that I'd have something on my menu that would make people say, "You know, Röckenwagner has the best chocolate dessert." Now I do, and here it is.

Macaronnade

4 ounces bittersweet chocolate, broken into pieces

4 tablespoons unsalted butter

1 teaspoon instant coffee crystals

4 large eggs, separated

¹/₂ cup granulated sugar

¹/₂ cup heavy whipping cream

2 tablespoons passion fruit juice (see Note)

2 teaspoons superfine sugar

Macaronnade. Preheat the oven to 300°. Butter six 5- or 6-ounce soufflé dishes and evenly coat them with granulated sugar, shaking the excess from one into the other until all are coated. Set aside.

In the top of a double boiler over gently simmering water, melt the chocolate and the butter together, stirring occasionally, until smooth. Stir in the coffee crystals and remove from the heat. In another bowl, beat the egg yolks together with the sugar until the mixture is pale and holds a ribbon when the beater is lifted away. In a third bowl, using perfectly clean beaters, beat the egg whites to stiff peaks. Fold the yolk mixture into the slightly cooled chocolate, then stir in one-quarter of the egg whites to loosen the mixture. Fold in the remaining whites, being careful not to deflate the mixture.

Put a kettle of water on to boil. Pour the mixture into the prepared soufflé dishes, filling each up to one-quarter inch from the rim, then run a finger around the inside of each rim to free the top of the soufflés from the ramekins and allow them to rise evenly. Place the dishes in a roasting pan. Pour the boiling water into the roasting pan so that it comes halfway up the sides of the ramekins to make a water bath (bain-marie). Place the roasting pan on the stovetop. Bring the water to a simmer, then bake in the oven for about 30 minutes, or until the soufflés have risen at least 1¹/₂ inches above the rim.

While the soufflés are baking, combine the whipping cream, passion fruit juice, and sugar in a mixing bowl and beat to soft peaks. Remove the soufflés from the oven and place on dessert plates lined with a small napkin to keep the ramekins from sliding. Scoop a small hole out of the center of each soufflé and fill with a dollop of the whipped cream mixture. Serve immediately.

Note: When passion fruit are in season, I recommend making your own passion fruit juice. To do so, simply collect and strain the juice that runs off when you open and slice the passion fruit. Each passion fruit yields about 2 tablespoons of juice.

Ready-made unsweetened passion fruit juice, which is very sour, is sometimes available frozen. If you do find frozen unsweetened passion fruit juice, you can intensify the flavor by reducing it by half and using as directed. If you must use regular store-bought passion fruit juice that has been sweetened, add 1 teaspoon of lemon juice for each tablespoon of the juice.

Warm Chocolate Tartlets with Espresso Sauce, Lemon Confit, and Hazelnut Parfait

Yield: 6 servings

This recipe has been published several times, and it even made the cover of Fine Cooking. *Don't feel that you must make every part of this recipe; its components are versatile and work well on their own or when combined. You can serve the chocolate tart with store-bought vanilla ice cream. The espresso sauce can be used as a topping for ice cream (but note that it must be made hours in advance), and the lemon confit is a great garnish for nearly any dessert. Even the hazelnut parfait can be served on its own. When the recipe was published in the* L.A. Times *recently, the writer said, "This...has 1000 calories per serving, but you lose 600 when you make it." It's our most popular dessert.*

Lemon Confit

2 lemons

1 orange

$^1/_2$ cup granulated sugar

$^1/_4$ cup water

1 tablespoon light corn syrup

Espresso Sauce

2 large egg yolks

$^1/_4$ cup sugar

1 cup heavy cream or $^1/_2$ cup milk and
   $^1/_2$ cup cream

1 teaspoon very finely ground espresso beans

Hazelnut Parfait

$^1/_2$ cup sugar

6 large egg yolks

$^3/_4$ cup coarsely chopped toasted
   hazelnuts (page 203)

1$^1/_3$ cups heavy cream

Chocolate Tartlets

9 ounces semisweet chocolate (preferably
   Valrhona, Caillebaut, or another Belgian, French,
   or Swiss chocolate), coarsely chopped

4 tablespoons unsalted butter, cut into
   $^1/_2$-inch cubes

Pinch of salt

6 large egg yolks

Scant $^1/_3$ cup sugar

2 large egg whites

6 large strawberries, thinly sliced lengthwise

6 sprigs of mint

6 Hazelnut Tuiles (page 172), optional

1 tablespoon confectioners sugar

Confit. Using a sharp, swivel-bladed vegetable peeler, remove the rind from the lemons and orange in strips, then trim away any remaining white pith on the back of each strip. Cut the strips into $^1/_8$-inch julienne. Place the julienne in a small saucepan and cover with cold water. Bring the water to a boil, then drain. Return the julienne to the pan and repeat the process two times. (This is called "triple-blanching.") Drain briefly on paper towels.

In a clean saucepan, combine the sugar, water, and corn syrup and stir gently over low heat until the sugar dissolves. Add the blanched citrus peel and bring the liquid to a simmer, then simmer until the citrus peels are tender but not breaking apart. The syrup should still be fairly liquid. Store the confit in a covered glass or ceramic bowl in the refrigerator until ready to serve. (The confit will keep, tightly covered, for up to 2 months.)

Sauce. In the bowl of a heavy-duty electric mixer, combine the egg yolks and sugar. Beat until the mixture is pale yellow and will hold a ribbon for 3 seconds when the beaters are lifted away. Fill a large bowl with ice and water, nest a smaller bowl inside it, and set aside on the counter. In a medium saucepan, gently heat the cream, stirring, just until it comes to a boil. Remove from the heat and stir in the ground espresso beans. Gradually fold half of the hot cream into the egg mixture, incorporating it well. Return the entire mixture to the saucepan containing the remaining cream. Return the pan to low heat and gently cook, stirring continuously just until the sauce thickens enough to coat the back of a spoon. Do not allow the sauce to boil. Immediately pour the hot sauce into the bowl set over the ice, and stir every few minutes until it is cool. (If there are any lumps in the sauce, strain it through a fine sieve to remove them.) Refrigerate for at least 2 hours or up to 24 hours before using.

Parfait. In the bowl of a heavy-duty electric mixer, combine the sugar and egg yolks. Beat until pale yellow and the mixture will hold a ribbon when the beaters are lifted away. Fold in the hazelnuts. In a separate bowl with clean beaters, beat the cream to soft peaks, then gently fold into the hazelnut mixture. Scoop the mixture into six 4-ounce ramekins, cover each with plastic wrap, and place in the freezer until frozen solid.

Tartlets. Butter and flour six 3-inch nonstick tartlet pans. Combine the chocolate, butter, and salt in a large bowl and set over a saucepan of gently simmering water. Stir occasionally until the chocolate is melted and the butter is well incorporated. Allow the mixture to cool until it is just slightly warm.

In the bowl of a heavy-duty electric mixer, combine the egg yolks and a scant 2 tablespoons of the sugar and beat on high until the mixture will hold a ribbon when the beater is pulled away.

Using a rubber spatula, fold the egg yolk mixture into the warm chocolate mixture.

Thoroughly clean the mixing bowl and beaters. (If there is any trace of fat left on them, the egg whites will not achieve their maximum loft.) Beat the egg whites with the remaining sugar to stiff peaks. Stir one-quarter of the egg whites into the chocolate mixture to loosen it. Gently fold the remaining whites into the mixture, making sure that it is evenly blended but taking care not to deflate it. Spoon the batter into the prepared tartlet pans, filling them up to 1/2 inch from the top. Place the tarts on a tray, cover with plastic wrap, and refrigerate for up to 6 hours.

When ready to serve, preheat the oven to 400°. Transfer the tartlets directly from the refrigerator to the oven and bake for 6 to 8 minutes, or until the top is slightly cracked and cakelike but the inside is still runny. Holding a tartlet in one hand in an ovenproof mitt, run a knife around the inside of the tartlet pan to loosen the tart, then turn it onto a serving plate. Make a small pool of Espresso Sauce next to the tart. Repeat with the remaining five tartlets. Dip the bottoms of the ramekins of Hazelnut Parfait in a bowl of hot water for 3 seconds or roll each ramekin between your hands to warm it slightly. Run a sharp knife around the inside edge of the ramekins to loosen the parfait, then invert each ramekin over the palm of your hand and slide the parfait onto the center of the espresso sauce. Fan a sliced strawberry next to the sauce. Place a teaspoonful of Lemon Confit on top of each tart. Garnish with a sprig of mint and a Hazelnut Tuile and dust the whole plate with confectioners sugar. Serve immediately.

Strawberry Pizza with Almond Cream

Yield: 4 servings

Most people put strawberries on tarts after the pastry is cooked. I like to cook the strawberries because I think they have a delightful flavor when warm, which is concentrated as they lose moisture during baking. A nice, easy variation is to make an apple pizza: simply replace the strawberries with 2 apples, very thinly sliced and fanned evenly over the surface.

Frangipane

1/4 **cup unsalted butter, softened**

1/3 **cup superfine sugar**

2 **large egg yolks**

1/4 **teaspoon almond extract, or**
   1 **tablespoon Amaretto**

1 **cup finely ground blanched almonds**
   (almond meal)

1 **tablespoon all-purpose flour**

Pizzas

1 **pound fresh or thawed frozen puff pastry**

2 **pints whole strawberries, stemmed**

1 **large egg yolk**

4 **sprigs mint**

Confectioners sugar

1 **pint best-quality vanilla ice cream**

Frangipane. In the bowl of a heavy-duty electric mixer, beat the butter and sugar until light and fluffy, scraping down the bowl as necessary. Add the egg yolks, beat well, then add the almond extract. Remove the beater and stir in the almonds and flour until evenly blended. The mixture should be the consistency of a thick paste.

Pizzas. Preheat the oven to 400°. On a lightly floured surface, roll out the pastry to a 1/8 inch thickness and, using a plate or cardboard circle as a template, with a very sharp knife cut four 7-inch circles. Transfer to two Teflon baking sheets or baking sheets lined with parchment paper. Spread a circle of frangipane in the center of each, leaving a 1-inch border. Place the strawberries stem end down on the frangipane. (They should be touching each other so that you can fit as many as possible onto the circles of frangipane.) Beat the egg yolk lightly with a fork and brush the border of the pastry with it. (Try not to let any yolk dribble down onto the cut sides of the pastry, otherwise it will not rise as high.) Bake the tartlets for 20 minutes, until the edges are golden and the pastry is baked through. Place a sprig of mint in the center of each pizza and dust them lightly with confectioners sugar. Serve hot with a scoop of vanilla ice cream.

Fresh Berry Gratin with Almond Croquant Parfait

Yield: 6 servings

This is one of my oldest desserts, and it is still one of our most popular. To me, and to many of my regular customers, this is one of those desserts with a distinct Röckenwagner flair. The technique of browning the desserts under the broiler may sound tricky, but as long as you watch closely it's easy. Just remove the plate from under the broiler if the crème begins to burn. Always be cautious when making caramel; when it's cooked at the right temperature it's hot enough to cause a serious burn.

Parfait

5 tablespoons water

5 tablespoons sugar

Scant ¹/₂ cup (3 ounces) blanched sliced
  almonds, toasted (page 203)

³/₄ cup confectioners sugar

4 large egg yolks

2 cups whipping cream

1 teaspoon pure vanilla extract

Crème Anglaise

2 cups whipping cream

¹/₂ vanilla bean, split

5 large egg yolks

5 tablespoons sugar

16 fresh strawberries, hulled and thinly sliced

1¹/₂ cups fresh raspberries

1¹/₂ cups fresh blackberries

³/₄ cup gooseberries

Sprigs of fresh mint, for garnish

Parfait. Lightly oil a baking sheet. In a small, very clean, heavy saucepan, combine the water and sugar and stir over low heat until the sugar has dissolved and the liquid appears clear. Increase the heat to high and cook the mixture until syrupy and golden brown. Be careful not to overcook and burn the caramel. If the mixture appears to be burning, decrease the heat to medium-high. If crystals form on the sides of the pan, remove them by swirling the liquid in the pan; never stir the caramel with an utensil. Add the almond slices, swirl to mix, and remove from the heat. Immediately pour the mixture onto the prepared sheet and let cool until brittle. Transfer to a cutting board and, with a sharp, heavy knife, chop coarsely.

Line the base of a 12 x 8-inch baking pan with parchment paper and set aside. In the top of a double boiler over gently simmering water, combine the confectioners sugar and egg yolks, whisking continuously for 4 to 5 minutes, or until the mixture will hold a ribbon when the whisk is lifted away. Remove from the heat and let cool for 5 minutes. In another bowl, whip the cream and vanilla to soft peaks. With a large rubber spatula, gently fold the yolk mixture into the whipped cream, then fold in the chopped almond candy. Pour the mixture into the prepared baking pan, cover, and freeze until solid, about 6 hours.

continued

Fresh Berry Gratin *continued*

Chocolate Bread Pudding

Crème Anglaise. In a medium, heavy saucepan, combine the whipping cream and vanilla bean and bring to a boil. Remove from the heat, cover, and let steep for 10 minutes. In a large stainless steel bowl, beat the egg yolks and sugar until pale and thickened. Gradually whisk the hot cream into the yolk mixture. Set the bowl of custard mixture over a medium saucepan of gently simmering water and stir continuously with a wooden spoon until the mixture thickens enough to coat the back of the spoon. Strain the mixture through a fine sieve into a clean bowl and refrigerate until chilled.

Preheat a broiler to high heat. With a sharp knife, cut the frozen parfait into six 4 x 4-inch squares. Place a parfait square in the center of each of 6 ovenproof dessert plates. Cover the parfait with sliced strawberries, top with a layer of raspberries, blackberries, and gooseberries, then spoon some of the crème anglaise over the berries. Place 2 dessert plates at a time under the broiler until the crème anglaise is golden brown and bubbly. Turn the plates once or twice so that the gratins brown evenly. Garnish the plates with mint sprigs and serve immediately.

Yield: 6 servings

This bread pudding is a bit more sophisticated than the more common homey, rustic versions.

6 (³⁄₄-inch-thick) slices brioche bread, cut into
  ³⁄₄-inch cubes and toasted until golden
¹⁄₄ cup firmly packed brown sugar
¹⁄₃ cup raisins
¹⁄₃ cup (about 2 ounces) semisweet
  chocolate chips
Zest of 1 orange
2 tablespoons chocolate liqueur plus
  additional, for garnish
2 large eggs, lightly beaten
1¹⁄₂ cups milk
1 cup whipping cream
¹⁄₂ teaspoon pure vanilla extract
6 scoops vanilla ice cream

In a large mixing bowl, combine the brioche, brown sugar, raisins, chocolate chips, and orange zest and toss to mix. Add the chocolate liqueur and mix again. In a separate mixing bowl, combine the eggs, milk, cream, and vanilla, whisking with a fork until well blended. Pour the wet ingredients over the bread mixture and toss until the bread is evenly moistened. Cover and refrigerate for 1 hour.

Preheat the oven to 325°. Cut out a 9-inch circle of parchment paper. Brush the bottom and sides of a 9-inch cake pan with flavorless vegetable oil, then press the paper onto the bottom of the pan. Brush the top of paper with a little more oil. Pour the bread mixture into the prepared pan and bake for 55 to 65 minutes, or until the mixture pulls away from the sides of the pan. Let cool for 5 to 10 minutes. Serve warm with a scoop of vanilla ice cream and chocolate liqueur drizzled over the top.

Mummy's Cheesecake

Yield: Serves 10

This truly tremendous cheesecake is a salute to my former mother-in-law, Sally Fama. Just follow the recipe and you will end up with a cheesecake you'll make over and over again. The sour cream topping is a great contrast to the very sweet and traditional cheesecake underneath. This cake is great for birthdays, because it is snow white and easy to write on.

Crust

1½ cups graham cracker crumbs

3 tablespoons sugar

Scant teaspoon ground cinnamon

7 tablespoons unsalted butter, melted

Filling

1 pound cream cheese

1 cup mascarpone (see Note)

⅓ cup sugar

2 teaspoons pure vanilla extract

3 large eggs, lightly beaten

Sour Cream Topping

1 cup sour cream

1½ tablespoons sugar

½ teaspoon pure vanilla extract

Crust. In a medium mixing bowl, combine the crumbs, sugar, cinnamon and enough of the butter to just bind the mixture. Use the remaining butter to thoroughly grease the bottom and sides of a 10-inch springform pan. Turn the pan on its side and add one-third of the crumb mixture. Press the crumbs with your fingertips around the sides of the pan, turning it as you go to make an even crust that reaches about two-thirds of the way to the rim. Set the pan down flat, add the remaining two-thirds of the crumb mixture, and press it with your fingertips into the corners and evenly across the base of the pan.

Filling. Preheat the oven to 300°. In the bowl of a heavy-duty electric mixer, combine the cream cheese, mascarpone, sugar, and vanilla and beat until light and fluffy. Add the eggs and beat until smooth. Pour the filling into the prepared crust.

Bake for 25 to 30 minutes, or until the center is firm.

Topping. While the cake is baking, whisk together the sour cream, sugar, and vanilla.

Leaving the oven on, remove the cheesecake and cool in the pan on a rack for 30 minutes. Slowly pour the topping over the top of the cake in an even layer, pouring it around the edges first and letting the topping spread to the center. Return to the oven and bake for an additional 10 minutes, or just until firm. Cool to room temperature, then chill overnight. Release the sides of the springform pan and transfer, along with the base, to a serving platter. Cut the cheesecake at the table.

Note: Mascarpone is an Italian cream cheese which has recently become widely available in the United States. It is a little sweeter and lighter than domestic cream cheese. If you are unable to find it, you can produce an acceptable substitute by combining the following ingredients in a food processor and processing until smooth: 12 ounces cream cheese, ¼ pound ricotta cheese, 2 tablespoons heavy cream, 1 tablespoon sugar, and the juice of 1 lemon. Refrigerate until needed (up to 1 week).

Gingered Pear Strudel with Almond Cream

Yield: 6 servings

Fresh ginger has played a big part in my cooking for the last 2 or 3 years, particularly because of my semirecent love affair with Asian food. This dessert is in no way Asian, but I find that ginger adds a welcome tangy bite to soft fruit desserts. The ginger flavor here is quite subtle, so ginger lovers might like to thinly slice some candied ginger and place it inside the strudel packages for a more intense hit of ginger.

Pears

4 cups water

1 cup granulated sugar

1½-inch length fresh ginger, peeled and
    sliced ½ inch thick

1 vanilla bean, split

3 Williams or other sweet, firm pears, peeled

Almond Cream

¾ cup slivered blanched almonds

1 cup confectioners sugar

½ cup unsalted butter, softened

⅓ cup all-purpose flour

2 large eggs

½ tablespoon dark rum

½ pound phyllo pastry, thawed

½ cup clarified butter, melted (page 202)

6 scoops chocolate sorbet or vanilla ice cream

Pears. In a saucepan large enough to hold all the pears snugly, combine the water, sugar, ginger, and vanilla bean. Stir over low heat until the sugar has dissolved and then increase the heat and bring to a simmer. Add the pears and poach for 15 to 20 minutes, turning occasionally so that they are evenly covered with syrup. The pears should be tender enough to be easily pierced with a toothpick; the cooking time will depend on their ripeness. Let cool, then refrigerate.

Almond Cream. In a food processor, pulse the almonds and sugar just until finely ground. Do not overprocess. In the bowl of a heavy-duty mixer, cream the butter until smooth and fluffy. Sift the almond powder and flour over the top and continue to beat until smooth and fluffy. Beat in the eggs, one at a time, incorporating the first one before adding the second. Add the rum and mix thoroughly.

Preheat the oven to 400°. Lightly oil a large baking sheet. Cut the poached pears in half and scoop out the cores. Thinly slice each half lengthwise and set aside, keeping the halves in their original shape.

Unroll the phyllo and cut it into three 4-inchwide stacks. Lay one strip on the work surface. Cover the remaining strips with a damp kitchen towel. Brush the strip with melted butter, and repeat until you have a stack 6 strips high. Repeat until you have 6 stacks of buttered phyllo strips. Using a spatula, spread a layer of almond cream ¼ inch thick on the top layer of each phyllo stack. Slightly fan out a pear half on one end of each stack and fold the other end of the stack over 1½ times to enclose the pear and form a flat strudel package. Brush the outside of the strudel with butter and transfer to the prepared baking sheet. Repeat with the remaining 5 pear halves and phyllo stacks. (At this stage the strudels can be covered with plastic wrap and refrigerated for up to 12 hours before baking.)

Bake the strudels for 10 to 15 minutes, or until golden and crispy. Cut them in half and place cut side up in the center of each of 6 dessert plates. Place a scoop of chocolate sorbet on the side and serve immediately.

Schwarzwälder Kirschtorte (Black Forest Cake)

Yield: 6 to 8 servings

This recipe uses a lot of alcohol, but that's its charm. It gets even better after it sits a few hours or days. The genoise is easier to cut into layers after it has rested at room temperature for 1 day.

Chocolate Genoise

²/₃ **cup all-purpose flour**

1 **teaspoon baking powder**

²/₃ **cup unsweetened cocoa powder**

4 **large eggs**

¹/₂ **cup superfine sugar**

Filling

1 **pound sour cherries, in juice**

2 **teaspoons water**

2 **teaspoons cornstarch**

3 **tablespoons granulated sugar**

¹/₂ **stick cinnamon**

3 **cups whipping cream**

¹/₄ **cup sugar**

2 **tablespoons kirschwasser (cherry schnapps)**

1 **tablespoon Simple Sugar Syrup (page 192)**

Block of chocolate for shaving, optional

Genoise. Preheat the oven to 350°. Butter and flour a deep, straight-sided 9-inch round cake pan well and set aside. Sift the flour, baking powder, and cocoa powder into a mixing bowl and set aside. In a large stainless steel mixing bowl, combine the eggs and sugar. Set the bowl over a saucepan of gently simmering water and whisk until the mixture has doubled in volume and is very pale. The mixture should hold a ribbon for a few seonds when the whisk is lifted away. Remove the bowl from the heat and continue whisking for 5 minutes to completely cool and stabilize the mixture. Quickly but gently fold in the sifted flour mixture. Pour the batter into the prepared pan and bake for 35 to 40 minutes, or until the cake is set and a toothpick

comes out clean when inserted in the center. Let rest for 5 minutes, then turn out onto a rack to cool completely.

Filling. Drain the cherries well, reserving their juice, and set aside. Combine the water and cornstarch, stirring until the cornstarch is dissolved. Measure 1 cup of the juice into a medium nonreactive saucepan. Add the sugar and cinnamon stick. Over medium heat, bring the mixture to a simmer, then remove the cinnamon stick and add the cornstarch mixture. Stir well and return to a boil. Gently fold the sour cherries into the syrup mixture until all the cherries are evenly coated. Bring the mixture just to a simmer, then remove 16 uniformly round cherries, and set aside to cool.

Assembly. With a long sharp knife, slice the genoise horizontally into 3 even layers. In a medium bowl, whip the cream and the sugar to soft peaks. In a small bowl, whisk together the kirschwasser and sugar syrup. Place the least perfect genoise layer on a cake platter and top with the cherry mixture, spreading it out to the edges. Place the next genoise layer on top, matching up the edges, and press it gently down onto the cherries. Brush the second layer generously with the kirschwasser mixture. Spread one-third of the whipped cream on top. Place the last (most perfect) layer of genoise on top, matching up the edges. Again brush with the kirschwasser mixture, then spread with a little less than one-third of the remaining whipped cream. Spread more whipped cream around the sides, reserving enough to pipe rosettes. Finally, using a pastry bag fitted with a star tip, pipe 16 rosettes equidistant around the top edge of the cake and place one of the reserved cherries in the center of each. Garnish the center of the cake with chocolate shavings. Refrigerate at least 3 hours or up to 2 days before serving.

John Sedlar's Corn Soufflés with Passion Fruit Whipped Cream

Yield: 6 servings

John Sedlar once made this for me when he was executive chef/owner of Abiquiu in Santa Monica, and I absolutely loved it. He graciously agreed to let me include it in this book, and if you try it you'll see why I think it is so wonderful. I've always loved soufflés, and I'm glad they're making a comeback. The passion fruit whipped cream spooned in at the end seeps into the light and airy soufflé mixture with splendid results.

Passion Fruit Whipped Cream
¼ cup passion fruit juice (see Note)
½ cup whipping cream

Soufflés
3 large ears fresh corn
¼ cup milk
½ vanilla bean, split
1 large egg yolk
2 tablespoons granulated sugar
Pinch of salt
2 tablespoons all-purpose flour

7 large egg whites
1 cup granulated sugar
1 tablespoon confectioners sugar

Whipped Cream. In a small saucepan, bring the passion fruit juice to a simmer and reduce it by half. Remove from the heat and let cool completely. In a chilled bowl, beat the cream to soft peaks and fold in the reduced passion fruit juice. Cover and refrigerate (up to 20 minutes).

Soufflés. With a sharp, heavy knife, cut the kernels off the ears of corn into a large bowl, along with any juice, then transfer them to a blender. Add the milk and blend at high speed, scraping down the sides of the container as necessary, until the mixture is smooth. Push through a fine strainer into a medium saucepan, pressing firmly on the solids to extract any remaining liquid. Discard the solids. You should have about 1 cup of liquid. Add the vanilla bean and bring the liquid to a simmer, stirring continuously to prevent the mixture from scorching. Remove from the heat.

In a large mixing bowl, combine the egg yolk, sugar, and salt and beat together until frothy. Sift the flour over the mixture, then fold it in. Gradually pour the warm corn liquid and milk over the yolk and flour mixture, whisking as you pour. Return the mixture to the saucepan and, over medium-low heat, bring just to a simmer while whisking continuously until very thick. Be sure to stir and scrape even the corners of the pan to be sure none of the mixture burns. Remove from the heat, strain the mixture through a fine sieve, and cool to room temperature before proceeding. (At this point, the base can be refrigerated for up to 2 days before continuing with the recipe.)

Thoroughly butter six 12-ounce soufflé dishes, making sure to butter the top rim. Dust with sugar, shaking out the excess, and place in a roasting pan large enough to hold them all without touching. Preheat the oven to 375°.

In a very large bowl, beat the egg whites to soft peaks. Sprinkle the sugar over the whites, and continue beating until stiff and glossy. Stir one-fourth of the egg whites into the soufflé base to loosen it, then thoroughly fold in the remaining whites, making sure not to deflate the mixture. Put a kettle of water on to boil.

Fill the prepared soufflé dishes with the mixture and run the back of a knife across the top to make it perfectly level. Run a finger around the inside rim of each soufflé dish (about $^1/_4$ inch deep) to free the top of the soufflés from the dishes and allow them to rise evenly. Fill the roasting pan with boiling water to come halfway up the sides of the soufflé dishes to make a water bath (bain-marie). Place the pan on the stovetop, and bring the water in the pan to a simmer. Transfer the roasting pan to the oven and bake for 20 to 25 minutes, or until the soufflés are well risen and the tops are golden. Remove from the oven and immediately make a small hole in the top of each soufflé with a teaspoon. Fill the holes with 1 tablespoon of the Passion Fruit Whipped Cream, dust with confectioners sugar, and serve immediately.

Note: When passion fruit are in season, I recommend making your own passion fruit juice. To do so, simply collect and strain the juice that runs off when you open and slice the passion fruit. Each passion fruit yields about 2 tablespoons of juice.

Ready-made unsweetened passion fruit juice, which is very sour, is sometimes available frozen. If you do find frozen unsweetened passion fruit juice, you can intensify the flavor by reducing it by half and using as directed. If you must use regular store-bought passion fruit juice that has been sweetened, add 1 teaspoon of lemon juice for each tablespoon of the juice.

Hazelnut Tuiles with Raspberry Soufflés and Crème Anglaise

Yield: 6 servings

This soufflé is quite easy. The key is a great-flavored, thick raspberry purée. You must adjust the sugar to taste depending on the ripeness of the raspberries, but it shouldn't be too sweet because there are other sweet flavors in the finished dish. These soufflés are very light and fluffy and do not fall as quickly as more traditional soufflés. There is nothing to weigh them down—they're only egg white. This recipe makes about 45 (3-inch diameter) tuiles, but the batter keeps for up to 2 weeks in the refrigerator, so you can make all the tuiles at once, or a few at a time. You'll find you have many uses for the leftover batter—the tuiles are perfect for molding into cups for sorbets or fruits or for layering. They turn any dessert into a sophisticated Napoleon.

Tuiles

$^1/_2$ **cup granulated sugar**

$^1/_2$ **cup corn syrup**

$^3/_4$ **cup finely chopped toasted hazelnuts (page 203)**

3 tablespoons unsalted butter

Raspberry Soufflés

3 pints ripe raspberries

3 tablespoons superfine sugar, or to taste

5 large egg whites

2 cups Crème Anglaise (page 165)

1 pint raspberries

1 pint golden raspberries or blackberries

$^1/_2$ **pint fraise de bois**

Tuiles. In the bowl of a heavy-duty electric mixer, combine all the ingredients and mix at medium-high speed for about 2 minutes, or until evenly blended. Cover the bowl with plastic wrap and refrigerate overnight or for up to 2 weeks.

Preheat the oven to 350° and lightly butter 1 or 2 nonstick baking sheets (only use a nonstick surface). Make $^1/_2$-inch balls out of the tuile mixture and set them 3 inches apart on the baking sheet. Bake until the balls have spread out perfectly flat and become crisp and golden around the edges. They will be a dark golden color, and very lacy and shiny. With a flat-ended metal spatula, remove the cookies one at a time. Immediately mold over a lime to make small cups or over an orange to make larger cups (depending on how many berries you will be serving). Working quickly, repeat until all cookies are molded. (Alternatively, mold the cookies over a rolling pin for a "taco" shape, or leave flat for Napoleons.) Remove the cookies from their mold as soon as they have cooled.

Soufflés. Thoroughly butter six 7-ounce ramekins, making sure to butter the top rim. Dust with sugar, shaking out the excess, and place in a roasting pan large enough to hold them all without touching. Preheat the oven to 375°.

In a food processor, purée the raspberries for about 1 minute, scraping down the sides of the bowl as necessary. Add 1 to 3 tablespoons of sugar and purée again until completely mixed. The purée should be very thick and smooth. In a large mixing bowl, beat the egg whites for about 30 seconds, or until frothy. Add 1 tablespoon of the sugar and continue beating the whites until soft peaks form. Strain the raspberry purée through a fine sieve into a large bowl. Stir one-quarter of the egg whites into the purée to lighten it, then gently fold in the remaining whites. Be careful not to deflate the mixture. Put a kettle of water on to boil.

Fill the prepared ramekins with the mixture and run the back of a knife across the top to make it perfectly level. Run a finger around the inside rim of each ramekin (about $^1/_4$ inch deep) to free the top of the soufflés from the ramekins and allow them to rise evenly. Fill the roasting pan with boiling water to come halfway up the sides of the ramekins to make a water bath (bain-marie). Place the pan on the stovetop, and bring the water to a simmer. Transfer the roasting pan to the oven and bake for about 10 minutes, or until the soufflés are well risen and the tops are golden.

Place a tuile on each of 6 serving plates and place a soufflé on the other side of the plates. With a tablespoon, immediately scoop out a small circle from the top of each soufflé and fill with about 2 tablespoons of the crème anglaise. Perch the spoon, cupped side down, on top of the soufflé. Mound about 6 tablespoons of raspberries in the tuiles. Spoon a little more crème anglaise around the edge of the plates and serve immediately.

In the Kitchen with the Kids

My three kids are very interested in food and know a lot about it (even though they share their school-mates' insatiable affection for pizza and Kraft Macaroni and Cheese!). I'm proud that they like to order off the menu whenever they come into the restaurant and don't want specially made simple dishes. At the tender ages of three, four, and eight, I don't expect them to want to eat fancy food all the time, but I am delighted that they already have an appreciation for great-tasting ingredients, beautiful presentation, and painstak-ing, classical preparation.

Gina, the eldest, is very open-minded and thought-ful about the food she eats. She can tell you about certain ingredients and orders her steak medium-rare. Hansi, the little one, is an adventurous eater—he'll try just about anything—and Roxy, the one in the middle, enjoys her reputation as an occasionally picky eater (sound familiar?). At home, like most other seasoned parents, I understand that when they're ready to eat, they're really ready, and I can't start preparing something interesting just then or they will have raided the refrigerator and filled up before it's on the table.

Although both their mother and I are chefs, we've made sure the kids know they'll never have to work in a restaurant kitchen unless they want to. Gina recently received a child's cookbook and has started to try some of the recipes at home, which is great fun. Time will tell whether Roxy and Hansi will also be interested enough to experiment in the kitchen as they grow older. But whatever career each of them chooses, I get satisfaction from knowing they'll always value good food, fine cook-ing, and shared meals.

Red Wine–Poached Figs on Pear Compote with Passion Fruit Whipped Cream

Yield: 6 servings

This dish features a tremendous combination of fruit and wine flavors. I think it tastes best with the pear compote and the figs at room temperature and the whipped cream, of course, nice and cold. One variation for the adventurous is to make this into a layered Napoleon using three Hazelnut Tuiles (page 172) for each serving. These figs are also very nice served alongside a wedge of cheese, and the pears make a wonderful topping for waffles or pancakes at a sophisticated brunch.

Figs

18 large or 24 small figs

3 cups dry red wine

$^1/_2$ cup sugar

Pear Compote

6 large yellow pears, peeled, seeded and cut into $^1/_2$-inch dice

1 vanilla bean, split

2 star anise

$^1/_3$ cup fruity white wine

2 tablespoons sugar or to taste

Passion Fruit Whipped Cream

$^1/_2$ cup whipping cream

2 tablespoons passion fruit juice (see Note)

6 flat Hazelnut Tuiles (page 172) for garnish

Figs. Preheat the oven to 325°. Cut off the stem and about $^1/_2$ inch of the top of each fig. Cut a shallow cross into the top of each, cutting down about one-third of the way into the center. In a large, nonreactive saucepan, combine the red wine and sugar over low heat and stir until the sugar has dissolved. Increase the heat to high and simmer until the liquid is reduced to three-fourths of its original volume. Place the figs in a large ceramic or glass baking dish that will hold them snugly in one layer. Pour the hot wine into the dish (it should reach about halfway up the sides of the figs).

Bake for 1 hour 15 minutes to 1$^1/_2$ hours, or until the figs are tender but not mushy. Remove from the oven and set aside. (The figs can be cooled and refrigerated for up to 8 hours. Return to room temperature before continuing.)

Compote. In a medium skillet, combine the pears, vanilla bean pod and seeds (scrape the seeds from the inside of the bean into the pan), star anise, white wine, and sugar, adding more sugar as needed to sweeten the pears. Over medium-low heat, bring the liquid to a gentle simmer and cook, stirring occasionally, for 12 to 15 minutes, or until the pears are almost falling apart. Set aside. (The pears can be cooled and refrigerated for up to 8 hours. Return to room temperature before continuing.)

Passion Fruit Whipped Cream. In a chilled bowl, whip the cream almost until soft peaks form. Add the passion fruit juice and continue whipping until soft peaks form.

Remove the vanilla bean pod halves and the star anise from the pear compote. In each of 6 shallow dessert bowls, make a bed of the pear compote and place 3 large or 4 small figs on top. Top with a dollop of the whipped cream, garnish with a Hazelnut Tuile, and serve immediately.

continued

Red Wine–Poached Figs *continued*

Note: When passion fruit are in season, I recommend making your own passion fruit juice. To do so, simply collect and strain the juice that runs off when you open and slice the passion fruit. Each passion fruit yields about 2 tablespoons of juice.

Ready-made unsweetened passion fruit juice, which is very sour, is sometimes available frozen. If you do find frozen unsweetened passion fruit juice, you can intensify the flavor by reducing it by half and using as directed. If you must use regular store-bought passion fruit juice that has been sweetened, add 1 teaspoon of lemon juice for each tablespoon of the juice.

Ice Cream Sandwiches

Yield: 6 servings

I love to cut these sandwiches into small triangles and pass them on chilled trays toward the end of a stand-up cocktail party. It's wonderful to see the smiles of surprise as people take their first bite. As an after-dinner dessert, one variation is to serve them with several different dipping sauces, such as chocolate and raspberry.

Hazelnut Genoise
8 large eggs
1½ cups granulated sugar
1 cup all-purpose flour
1 cup finely ground toasted hazelnuts (page 203)
2 tablespoons Frangelico (hazelnut liqueur)

Parfait
5 tablespoons water
5 tablespoons granulated sugar
Scant ½ cup (3 ounces) sliced blanched almonds, toasted (page 203)
¾ cup confectioners sugar
4 large egg yolks
2 cups whipping cream
1 teaspoon pure vanilla extract

6 (½-inch-thick) pineapple rings

Genoise. Brush a 26 x 18-inch baking sheet with melted butter, line with parchment paper, and brush the paper with more butter. Sprinkle the paper evenly with flour and shake off the excess. Preheat the oven to 350°.

Place the whole eggs (in their shells) in a large bowl and cover with lukewarm water. Let warm for 10 minutes. Break the eggs into the bowl of a heavy-duty electric mixer and add the sugar. Beat for about 4 minutes, or until the mixture is pale and fluffy and will hold a ribbon when the beaters are lifted away.

Transfer one-third of the egg mixture to a large mixing bowl and pour the flour and ground hazelnuts through a sieve into the bowl. Fold in the flour and nuts. Return this mixture to the mixer bowl and fold all together. Again transfer one-third of the mixture to the large mixing bowl (there is no need to wash it before reusing) and fold in the Frangelico. Return to the mixer bowl and again gently fold together, taking care not to deflate the delicate mixture. Spread the mixture on the prepared baking sheet and bake for 15 to 20 minutes, or until lightly golden and springy. Do not allow it to get too crisp or it will crack. Cover with a kitchen towel to prevent it from drying out and cool in the pan on a rack.

Parfait. Lightly oil a baking sheet. In a small, very clean, heavy saucepan, combine the water and sugar and stir together over low heat until the sugar has dissolved and the liquid appears clear. Increase the heat to high and simmer until syrupy and golden brown. Be careful not to overcook and burn the caramel. If crystals form on the sides of the pan, remove them by swirling the liquid in the pan (never stir the caramel with a utensil). Add the toasted almonds, swirl to mix, and remove from the heat. Immediately pour the mixture onto the prepared baking sheet and let cool until quite brittle. Turn out the almond candy (croquant) onto a cutting board and, with a sharp, heavy knife, chop coarsely.

Line the bottom of a 12 x 8-inch baking pan with parchment paper and set aside. In a double boiler over gently simmering water, combine the confectioners sugar and egg yolks, whisking continuously for about 5 to 6 minutes, or until the mixture will hold a ribbon when the beaters are lifted away. Remove from the heat and continue whisking for 5 minutes more, until cool. In another bowl, whip the cream with the vanilla to soft peaks. With a large rubber spatula, gently fold the cooled yolk mixture into the whipped cream, then fold in the chopped almond candy.

Assembly. Place your hand on top of the genoise to steady it and, with a long, sharp knife, gently cut it in half horizontally. Place one half, browned side down, on a baking sheet. Gently spread the parfait quickly and evenly over the bottom half of the genoise, being careful not to tear it. Place the other half of the genoise, browned side up, on top of the parfait, matching up the edges. Cover with plastic wrap and transfer the sheet to the freezer. Freeze for at least 3 hours, or until frozen solid (up to 3 days) before serving.

Cut the sandwich into six 3 x 3-inch squares, then cut each in half diagonally, into triangles. Place a pineapple ring in the center of each of 6 dessert plates. Lean 2 triangles up against each pineapple ring, on either side, and serve immediately.

RÔCKENWAGNER BASICS

Spätzle

Yield: 6 servings

Spätzle is one of the first things I ever made and I never got tired of it. When I lived in Germany, there were times I virtually lived on spätzle alone. Spätzle are almost like dumplings, more similar to a rustic gnocchi than to pasta. They are a great vehicle for thick sauces and ragus, particularly those with beef, game, or veal. When I first arrived in America, most people I talked with had never heard of spätzle, but that is quickly changing. I would like to think I am partially responsible for the new interest in it, but who knows? Spätzle go on and off our menu, but people are beginning to ask for them when they are not on the menu. One nice variation is to add 2 teaspoons of finely chopped parsley or any fresh herb when you add the eggs to the flour; another is to add 1 tablespoon caraway seeds.

3 cups all-purpose flour
1 teaspoon salt
6 large eggs
4 tablespoons water

2 tablespoons unsalted butter
Salt and freshly ground black pepper to taste
3 tablespoons snipped chives or green onion tops,
    cut on the diagonal

In a large mixing bowl, combine the flour and salt and make a well in the center. In a small mixing bowl, whisk the eggs with the water, then pour them into the well. With a wooden spoon, begin stirring the egg mixture, incorporating a little flour each time you whisk, until you have a thick, wet, doughy mixture. Continue working the dough, lifting it up as you stir to incorporate air into the mixture and make it a little bubbly. It should be thick enough to cling to the spoon, then drop off.

Bring a large stockpot of salted water to a rapid boil. Form the spätzle using one of the methods described on the opposite page (see sidebar). Add the spätzle to the boiling water. When they rise to the surface, give them a gentle stir and cook for about 20 seconds. Drain briefly in a clean colander before tossing with the butter, salt, pepper, and chives. Serve immediately (see Note).

Note: If spätzle is not served immediately, remove it from the boiling water, shock in cold water, then drain and toss with 2 teaspoons of vegetable oil. When ready to serve, heat the butter in a large nonstick pan and add the salt, pepper, and chives. Add the spätzle and toss to coat well.

French Fries

Yield: 4 servings

When potatoes are newly harvested (in the spring and summer), the first frying process will take about 3 minutes. In fall and winter, when the potatoes have been stored for some length of time, the first frying will take 5 minutes. The keys to making puffy, nongreasy fries are double-frying and maintaining the oil at the correct temperature.

1½ **pounds russet potatoes, peeled and cut into** ¼-**inch batons**
3 **quarts vegetable oil**
Salt to taste

Rinse the potato batons thoroughly in cold running water. Transfer them to a double thickness of kitchen towels and dry well, taking care not to break them as you pat them dry.

In a deep-fryer, or large, heavy saucepan, heat the oil to 325°. Place the batons in a frying basket, submerge the basket in the hot oil, and fry for 3 to 5 minutes. The potatoes should be almost tender but not crisp or at all colored. Remove the basket from the oil and drain for 10 minutes while you increase the oil temperature to 375°. (If not serving immediately, the fries can be cooled to room temperature after they drain and refrigerated for up to 2 days.) Again submerge the fries in the basket and cook until crisp and just beginning to turn golden. (Do not over-fry or they will be greasy.) Transfer to a double thickness of paper towels, sprinkle with salt, and serve immediately.

Spätzle

Spätzle is served in virtually every restaurant in southern Germany, and can accompany any kind of meat, goulash, or poultry dish. It is especially good with game and is never served with fish. Like rice in Mexico or *frites* in France, it is the most common form of starch in southern Germany. (In northern Germany, however, you are more likely to find potatoes on the plate.)

In my parents' restaurant, spätzle-making was one of the biggest jobs, but it was an important one because restaurants were measured by the quality of their spätzle. I inherited this job practically as soon as the restaurant opened, when I was only 12. It was a privilege, but also a chore. Every day or so, I had to make a big 50-egg batch, because we served it with almost everything. Some restaurants cheated by making their spätzle with fewer eggs, but you could always tell—not just by the flavor, but also by the color. (In Germany, eggs were yellow and actually tasted like eggs, which I've found less common in this country.)

There are several ways to form spätzle. The old-fashioned German way is to use a cutting board, spreading the dough flat on the board, then cutting little ribbons off the edge with a flat spatula and pushing them into rapidly boiling, salted water. The other method uses a spätzle press, which is similar to a potato ricer but has larger and fewer holes. In fact, it looks like a giant garlic press. Using a press, the dough is extruded and cut into the boiling water. Spätzle presses are now available from several retailers in this country (see page 204), and they certainly simplify the process. Alternatively, a colander with large (³/₈-inch) holes can be substituted for the press. Just push the mixture through the holes with a large metal spoon. Spätzle can easily be "held" after cooking for several hours. Just add a tiny amount of oil—not too much or the spätzle will be too oily to hold the sauce—after it has thoroughly drained. And don't worry if the spätzle clumps together a little while it waits; you can easily break it up when you reheat it. Spätzle can be refrigerated, but it absorbs other flavors like a sponge, so be sure to cover the container tightly.

Pretzel Knödel

Yield: 12 knödel

*Traditional German knödel is made from stale
dinner rolls. This is my updated version, which uses
soft pretzels instead. The pretzels give the knödel a
very distinct flavor, and I think it makes a unique
side dish—it's difficult to pinpoint the flavor if you
don't know what's in it. It is easiest to make this
knödel in larger quantities, but it freezes well and
makes a convenient last-minute accompaniment for
duck, poultry, and veal.*

½ cup milk

¼ cup unsalted butter

2 small or 1 medium yellow onion,
  coarsely chopped

⅓ cup coarsely chopped flat-leaf parsley

6 ounces unsalted soft pretzels (page 142),
  cut into ¾-inch cubes

3 large eggs, lightly beaten

1 teaspoon salt

½ teaspoon freshly ground black pepper

Pinch of freshly ground nutmeg

2 tablespoons finely chopped parsley

In a small saucepan, heat the milk over low heat
until nearly simmering, then set aside. In a
medium skillet, heat 2 tablespoons of the butter
over medium-low heat. Add the onions and
sauté for 3 to 4 minutes, or until softened. Add
the parsley, stir together for 1 minute, then
remove from the heat and set aside.

Place the pretzel pieces in a large mixing bowl,
pour the warm milk over them, and stir to mix.
Add the eggs, mix well, and add the sautéed
onion, salt, pepper, and nutmeg. Stir the mixture
again and let sit for 5 minutes.

Turn half of the mixture out onto a 15-inch-long
piece of heavy-duty plastic wrap placed horizontally on the work surface. Spread the mixture
along the center of the plastic to form a roughly
even sausage shape about 8 inches long. Wrap
the long bottom edge of plastic up and over the
sausage, then bring the top edge up and over
the bottom edge, encasing the dough. While
holding the mixture in at one end, twist the
other end several times and tie a double knot
in it. Hold the sausage upright with the knotted
end down and let the mixture settle and compact, pressing out the excess air through the top
end while you hold it closed loosely enough for
the air to escape. Twist the top end several times
and tie a double knot in it. Cut off the excess
plastic at the ends and tie the sausage snugly
once in the center. Repeat the process with the
remaining mixture.

Fill a large rectangular roasting pan with water
and bring it to a simmer over medium heat. Add
the sausages and simmer for 25 minutes, or
until firm, turning them over halfway through
the cooking time. Cool to room temperature,
then chill. (At this point, 1 of the sausages can be
frozen for future use. When ready to use, thaw
for 1 hour at room temperature, then continue
with the recipe.)

Remove the plastic wrap, then slice the chilled
sausage with a serrated knife into ¾-inch
rounds. Heat the remaining 2 tablespoons butter
in a large nonstick skillet over medium-high
heat. Add the knödel and sauté for 2 minutes on
each side, or until golden. Sprinkle with the parsley and serve immediately, or within 5 minutes.

House-Cured Salmon

Yield: about 3 pounds

This salmon, which is my version of gravlax, is worth the trouble and should be made in a large quantity. If you do not plan to use it all at once, cut the cured salmon into 6-ounce pieces, wrap well, and freeze until needed. Or, cut all the quantities in half. Try marinating the salmon for only 36 hours, and then experiment with curing it for a longer period. If you let it marinate for more than 36 hours, it will pick up lovely strong flavors from the onions and celery.

Curing your own salmon costs approximately one-quarter as much as store-bought smoked salmon and is every bit as tasty and beautiful in hors d'oeuvres, mousses, brunch dishes, and salads. Or, simply serve slivers of it on slices of pumpernickel bread.

1 large white onion, coarsely chopped

1 large or 2 medium leeks, white and light green parts only, coarsely chopped

²/₃ cup coarsely chopped carrots

1 cup coarsely chopped dill

1 cup coarsely chopped flat-leaf parsley

1 small bunch chives, cut into 2-inch lengths (about 1 ounce)

Scant tablespoon dry mustard powder

1 teaspoon coriander seeds, crushed

1 teaspoon crushed red pepper flakes

1 teaspoon chile powder

2 tablespoons kosher salt

1¹/₂ tablespoons sugar

Juice of 2 limes

1 large side of salmon (about 3 pounds), all bones removed

In a food processor, combine the onions, leeks, carrots, dill, parsley, and chives and pulse until a rough paste forms. Transfer the mixture to a mixing bowl and add the spices, salt, sugar, and lime juice. Mix well to make a paste.

On a large work surface, lay a 4-foot-long piece of plastic wrap and spread half of the curing paste down the center in a flat, wide strip, keeping it at least 2 inches away from all the edges. Lay the salmon skin side down over the paste and spread the remaining paste over the flesh side of the fish. Fold in the edges of the plastic wrap, then lay another 4-foot piece of plastic over the top, tucking the edges of the top piece underneath to make an airtight seal. Place the wrapped salmon in a large roasting pan to catch any juices that leak out and refrigerate for at least 36 hours, turning over every 8 hours. (The salmon will keep this way for up to 1 week and the flavor will only improve. If you cure the salmon for longer than 36 hours, however, turn it every 24 hours.)

Unwrap the salmon and scrape off the curing paste, then rinse briefly to remove any excess paste. Pat dry and, flesh side up, slice very thinly on the diagonal with a long, razor-sharp knife. Use as directed.

Pickled Pumpkin

Yield: 2 quarts

This easy pickle is a wonderful condiment for chicken, squab, game hens—in fact, for any kind of meat or game. In the summer, make it with butternut squash.

1³/₄ pounds cubed pumpkin (³/₄-inch cubes)
1²/₃ cups white wine vinegar
1²/₃ cups water
2 walnut-sized pieces unpeeled fresh ginger, thinly sliced on the bias
1³/₄ cups sugar
1 teaspoon salt
5 cloves
14 whole black peppercorns

Thoroughly wash a 2-quart preserving jar with a fresh rubber gasket seal, and boil the jar for 10 minutes (without the gasket) to sterilize it. Place the cubed pumpkin in the jar and fit the gasket in place.

In a large saucepan, combine the vinegar, water, ginger, sugar, salt, cloves, and peppercorns. Over low heat, stir the mixture with a wooden spoon until the sugar has dissolved, then increase the heat to high and bring the mixture to a boil. Reduce the heat and simmer for 5 minutes, then pour the hot liquid over the pumpkin in the jar. Immediately seal the jar and let it cool to room temperature, then refrigerate for 1 week before using. Once unsealed, the pickled pumpkin will keep for 2 to 3 weeks in the refrigerator.

Pickled pumpkin (left back), Spätzle (left front), and Pretzel Knödel (right)

Home-Cured Tomatoes

Yield: 3 pounds

I still can't believe that people buy sundried toma-toes in a supermarket. We make our own in the oven, which is inexpensive and easy. Storing them in olive oil gives them a wonderful flavor and creates an aromatic oil that is great for sautéing and vinai-grettes. Depending on what you will be using them for, try adding a few cloves of slivered garlic to the oil. This recipe can be halved, doubled, or tripled.

½ cup extra virgin olive oil
Salt and freshly ground pepper
3 pounds ripe plum tomatoes, halved and cores
   removed if woody
2 teaspoons dried thyme or marjoram, crumbled
Extra virgin olive oil for storing, optional

Preheat the oven to 150° (see Note). Generously brush 2 baking sheets with 2 to 3 tablespoons of the olive oil and sprinkle them with salt and pepper. Arrange the halved tomatoes on the pan, cut side up, and brush them with the remaining olive oil. Sprinkle the cut sides with salt, pepper, and the herbs. Dry the tomatoes in the warm oven for 6 to 8 hours, or until they are shriveled and slightly golden, but still juicy, with a very deep and concentrated flavor. Store in an airtight container in the refrigerator for up to 1 week. If desired, cover the tomatoes with olive oil and store for up to 3 weeks.

Note: This low temperature is difficult for some ovens to maintain. Be sure to use an oven ther-mometer and, if the oven keeps climbing up to a higher temperature, prop the oven door open about an inch with a bunched-up kitchen towel.

Chicken Stock

Yield: about 1½ quarts

This is a basic chicken stock that can be used when-ever chicken stock is called for. If you have a large stockpot, you can double or even triple this recipe; just freeze the stock in 1 or 2 cup containers for future use.

2 quarts water
5 pounds uncooked chicken carcasses, wings,
   or assorted pieces
2 carrots, washed but unpeeled
2 ribs celery
1 leek, split and washed
1 yellow onion, peeled
½ head unpeeled garlic
10 white peppercorns, lightly crushed
1 sprig fresh thyme

In a large saucepan, combine the water and chicken pieces and bring to a slow simmer over medium heat. Skim the impurities from the surface with a large flat spoon, then add the carrots, celery, leek, onion, garlic, peppercorns, and thyme and simmer, partially covered and undisturbed, for 5 hours, adding water periodi-cally so that the ingredients are always covered.

Strain the stock through a strainer lined with a double thickness of slightly dampened cheese-cloth, let cool, then refrigerate overnight. Skim off and discard the fat from the top of the stock. Use the stock as directed, or freeze for future use.

Beef or Lamb Stock

Yield: 1 quart

I think this stock is much better when it's made with chicken stock instead of water, so try to use it if you can—whether you make your own or substitute a good-quality canned low-sodium broth. Ask your butcher to chop the bones into 1-inch pieces; smaller chunks give the stock a much better flavor than larger bones, and the whole process takes less time.

▶ **2 tablespoons olive oil**

3 to 4 pounds beef or lamb bones, chopped into 1- or 2-inch pieces

2 tablespoons tomato paste

1 carrot, coarsely chopped

1 yellow onion, coarsely chopped

4 cloves unpeeled garlic, crushed

2 sprigs fresh thyme

1 cup white wine

1½ quarts Chicken Stock (page 186) or water

Preheat the oven to 350°. Heat a heavy roasting or braising pan on the stovetop over medium-high heat. Add the oil and the bones to the pan and stir for 4 to 5 minutes, or until slightly browned. Transfer the pan to the oven and roast for 15 minutes, stirring halfway through the cooking time. Add the tomato paste, carrot, onion, and garlic to the pan and roast, stirring every few minutes so that the tomato paste does not scorch, for another 15 minutes, or until the vegetables and bones are well caramelized.

Transfer the bones and vegetables to a stockpot. On the stovetop over medium heat, add the thyme and wine to the roasting pan and deglaze, stirring and scraping the bottom and sides to release all of the flavorful bits, then continue to cook until the wine has almost evaporated. Transfer to the stockpot. Add the chicken stock and simmer, stirring occasionally, until the liquid is reduced by half, or until about 3 cups of liquid remain. Remove from the heat and strain through a strainer lined with a double thickness of slightly dampened cheesecloth, pressing down on the solids to extract all their flavor. Discard the solids and use the stock as directed, or freeze for future use.

Lobster Stock

Veal Demiglace

Yield: about 1½ quarts

Don't let the stock boil or it will have a slightly soapy taste. Get the lobster skeletons from your fishmonger, or freeze the shells from the lobsters you cook.

▶ 4 uncooked lobster skeletons, or 6 cooked shells
1 tablespoon olive oil
1 yellow onion, coarsely chopped
3 cloves garlic, coarsely chopped
3 tablespoons tomato paste
2 cups tomato juice
4 quarts water
1 tablespoon black peppercorns
1 small bay leaf

Wrap the lobster shells in an old kitchen towel and crush with a rolling pin into walnut-sized pieces. Drain the shells in a colander set over a bowl to catch the excess juices, and reserve the liquid.

In a large, heavy stockpot, heat the olive oil over medium-high heat. Add the lobster shells and stir for 5 minutes, or until slightly golden. Add the onion and the garlic and cook for 3 to 4 minutes more, or until the vegetables have begun to soften. Add the tomato paste and stir continuously for 2 minutes more. Add the tomato juice, water, peppercorns, bay leaf, and reserved lobster juices. Simmer the mixture, partially covered, over medium heat for 25 minutes.

Strain the stock through a colander into a clean pan, pressing firmly on the solids to extract any remaining liquid. Discard the solids. Bring the stock to a simmer and reduce to about one-third of its original volume, until a scant 6 cups of liquid remain. Strain through a sieve lined with two layers of slightly dampened cheesecloth. Use as directed, or freeze in 2-cup portions for up to 4 months.

Yield: 2 cups

Demiglace is one of the great building blocks of classic cuisine, and, in my opinion, it will never go out of style.

▶ 2 quarts Veal Stock (page 186)

In a medium saucepan, bring the stock to a simmer and reduce it to one-quarter of its original volume, about 2 cups of syrupy liquid, skimming off any foamy fat or impurities as you simmer. The process may take up to 45 minutes. The demiglace can be frozen in 1-cup quantities almost indefinitely.

Veal Stock

Yield: about 2 quarts

I worked in a restaurant in Lausanne that took stock-making to an extreme: we had squab stock, duck stock, veal stock, lamb stock, lobster stock, and crab stock, all simmering away at the same time. But it was the huge pot of veal stock that was the most carefully tended as we went about our daily routine. Veal stock continues to be one of the quintessential basics of fine cooking. Unfortunately, many restaurants now buy their veal stock in order to control increasing labor costs.

10 pounds veal knuckle bones
4 carrots, cut into 1-inch pieces
2 large yellow onions, cut into quarters
$\frac{1}{2}$ cup tomato paste

Preheat the oven to 400°. In a large roasting pan, roast the veal bones for $1\frac{1}{2}$ hours, turning them over every 30 minutes. Add the carrots and onions, stir together, and roast for 45 minutes more, or until all the bones and vegetables are nicely browned. Stir in the tomato paste and roast for 5 minutes more, then transfer all the ingredients to a large stockpot.

Pour off and discard the excess fat from the roasting pan. Set the pan over medium-low heat. Add 3 cups of water to the pan and deglaze it, stirring and scraping the bottom and sides to release all the flavorful bits. Pour the deglazing liquid over the bones and vegetables in the stockpot and add enough water to cover the ingredients by about 4 inches. Bring to a simmer over medium-low heat, then reduce the heat. Simmer gently, uncovered, for 7 to 8 hours, skimming off any fat and impurities that rise to the surface. Whenever the water falls below the top of the ingredients, add more to cover generously. At the end of the cooking time, the ingredients should still be covered by about 2 inches of liquid.

Strain the stock through a colander lined with a double thickness of slightly dampened cheesecloth, pressing firmly on the solids to extract any remaining liquid. Discard the solids. In a large, clean saucepan, reduce the liquid over medium-high heat to about two-thirds of its original volume. Use as directed, or freeze in 2-cup portions for up to 4 months.

The Essential Ingredient

Veal stock is the true grand dame of all stocks. In Europe, restaurants take great pride in making a good veal stock. Just as American restaurants are often judged by their Caesar salad, it's the quality of an establishment's veal stock and demiglace that matter in Europe.

What makes a good veal stock? Well, for one thing, lots of gelatin. The gelatin has no flavor, it simply adds body to the finished sauce. There is, however, too much of a good thing. Excess gelatin will give the stock a gummy texture. The flavor is achieved by using the right quantity of bones, a nice selection of vegetables, good wine, and the right amounts of water added at the right times. Luckily, veal stock is best made in large quantities (double or triple the recipe if you have a large stockpot) and freezes perfectly, so it's very much worth the effort. You'll be thankful you went to the trouble when you taste the difference in your sauces.

Quark Cheese

Yield: 2 to 2½ pounds

Quark is a popular baking cheese in Europe, but it is rarely available here. It is similar to cottage cheese but is more acidic and forms more of a solid mass rather than the small, individual curds in cottage cheese. It is easy to make, assuming you have a lot of space in your refrigerator. Besides the cheese's uses in baking, it's also a good appetizer when spiked with finely chopped garlic and shallot, cracked black pepper, and chopped fresh herbs.

2½ quarts whole milk
1 tablespoon cultured buttermilk
½ teaspoon salt

In a large bowl set over a saucepan of gently simmering water, heat the milk to 80°. Add the buttermilk and stir the mixture slowly and very thoroughly. Remove the bowl from the saucepan, cover with plastic wrap, and let rest at 65° to 70° for 24 hours. The milk should form a curd, a mass which is easily discernible from the clear, watery whey. If it has not, place the bowl over a pan of slightly warm water for 2 more hours.

Line a large colander with a double layer of dry cheesecloth and place the colander over a bowl. Gently ladle the curd into the colander, disturbing it as little as possible. Allow the curd to drain, covered with a pan lid or a towel, for 5 hours in the refrigerator.

Bring the four corners of the cheesecloth together and tie with long string, enclosing the curd completely. Hang the bag over the bowl in a cool place for 6 hours more, checking the curd every 2 or 3 hours to make sure it is an even texture throughout. If the curd on the outside of the bag is firmer, incorporate it into the center until the curd is evenly blended and re-hang the bag. Transfer the quark to a container and beat in the salt. Further beating will make the curd creamier.

Balsamic Reduction

Yield: about 1²/₃ cups

This is a very intense sauce that doesn't go with absolutely everything—it must accompany strongly flavored ingredients. Since you would never use very much of it, you could freeze it in ice cube trays and use one cube at a time to make an instant sauce for roasted meats or to flavor soups, stews, and other sauces.

3 cups Veal Stock (page 189)
2 cups balsamic vinegar

In a medium saucepan, reduce the veal stock to two-thirds of its original volume, about 2 cups.

At the same time, in a medium saucepan (preferably one wider at the rim than at the base to allow the liquid to evaporate faster), bring the vinegar to a rapid simmer and reduce it to one-fourth of its original volume, or until about ¹/₂ cup of syrupy liquid remains. Add the reduced stock and again reduce the mixture to two-thirds of its volume, so that 1²/₃ cups of liquid remain. Refrigerate in small quantities for up to 1 month, or freeze.

Shrimp Glaze

Yield: about 3 cups

This is another one of the building blocks in my kitchen. It keeps in the refrigerator for up to 2 weeks and is essential for avid barbecuers. Brush it on tuna and other shellfish, as well as on shrimp.

4 tablespoons prepared ketchup
2 tablespoons soy sauce
3 tablespoons white wine vinegar
1 tablespoon toasted sesame oil
4 tablespoons finely chopped garlic
2 tablespoons dry white wine
4 tablespoons grated or finely chopped
  fresh ginger
2 teaspoons sweet paprika
1 teaspoon ground cayenne pepper
²/₃ cup unsalted butter, cut into 10 pieces
  and softened

In a medium saucepan, combine all the ingredients and stir together over low heat until the butter has just melted. Remove from the heat and transfer to a blender. Blend for 1 minute, pulsing on and off and scraping down the sides of the container several times until the mixture is completely smooth. Use as directed, or cover and store in the refrigerator for up to 2 weeks.

Barbecue Sauce

Yield: 3½ cups

This is a very basic, straightforward barbecue sauce, even though there are a lot of ingredients. I use this sauce with the Hong Kong to L.A. Chicken Salad (page 34), which is fairly strong in flavor on its own. With a more delicate dish, I would step-down its power, reducing the paprika and more robust ingredients until the sauce complemented the dish perfectly.

▶ 1 yellow onion, finely chopped
1 clove garlic, minced
1 teaspoon salt
⅛ teaspoon freshly ground black pepper
½ teaspoon pure chile powder (such as pasilla chile powder)
½ teaspoon celery salt
½ teaspoon dry mustard
1 tablespoon Worcestershire sauce
¼ cup firmly packed brown sugar
¼ cup apple cider vinegar
16-ounce can tomato sauce or peeled tomatoes in their juices
½ cup tomato paste
Wedge of lemon
⅛ teaspoon Tabasco sauce

In a large nonreactive saucepan, combine all the ingredients over medium heat. Bring to a simmer (stir to break up the tomatoes if whole). Cover the pan and continue to simmer for about 20 minutes, or until the sauce has thickened. If you have used whole tomatoes, remove the lemon wedge and purée the sauce briefly in a blender. Strain through a fairly coarse sieve into a glass container. Cool and use as directed, or cover and refrigerate for up to 2 weeks.

Simple Sugar Syrup

Yield: ½ cup

A "simple syrup" is just that: equal amounts of sugar and water in any quantity. A versatile building block for patisserie, dessert, and cocktail making, it is commonly used in sorbet, brushed on layers of chocolate genoise for Black Forest cakes, and mixed with rum to make a soaking solution for the savarins in the classic dessert Baba au Rhum. Since sugar does not dissolve easily in cold water, sugar syrup is one of the only easy ways to sweeten lemonade, iced tea, cocktails, and wine punches. It is a very useful thing to have around the kitchen.

▶ ⅓ cup water
⅓ cup sugar

Combine the water and sugar in a small saucepan. Stir over low heat until the sugar has dissolved, then increase the heat to high and bring the mixture to a boil. Boil for 1 minute, then remove from the heat and let cool.

Honey-Mustard Dressing

Yield: about 2 cups

This is another versatile building block. It may have a lot of ingredients, but it is definitely a worth the labor. I like to make a simple salad of julienned carrots, cucumbers, and jicama and coat it lightly with this dressing. It also goes well with all types of seafood. The prepared hot Japanese mustard comes in a tube and can be found at Asian markets.

▶ 1 large egg
1½ teaspoons grated fresh ginger
½ clove garlic, finely chopped
1 tablespoon prepared hot Japanese mustard, or hot Asian dry mustard powder
2 tablespoons honey
2 tablespoons soy sauce
½ cup rice vinegar
¾ cup peanut oil
¼ cup toasted sesame oil

In a food processor, combine the egg, ginger, garlic, mustard, honey, and soy sauce and process until smooth, scraping down the sides of the bowl as necessary. Add the vinegar and process for a few seconds. With the motor running, drizzle in the peanut and sesame oils and process until emulsified. Store covered in the refrigerator for up to 2 days.

Balsamic Vinaigrette

Yield: ½ cup

Although this vinaigrette is "light" from a calorie standpoint, it is not "light" in flavor — the shallot and herbs give it quite a punch. Balsamic vinegar is much milder in acidity than red wine vinegar, so using half balsamic means you need less oil to make a balanced dressing. That's why when you use lemon juice as the acid in a dressing you need a larger ratio of oil to give a balanced flavor. Because of this, balsamic vinegar is actually quite good for the calorie-conscious cook.

▶ 2 teaspoons balsamic vinegar
2 teaspoons red wine vinegar
½ teaspoon salt
Pinch of freshly ground black pepper
¼ cup extra virgin olive oil
1 shallot, minced
1 tablespoon mixed chopped herbs (such as parsley, chives, or chervil), optional

In a small bowl or a mini food processor, combine the balsamic and the red wine vinegars, salt, and pepper. Whisk to blend and drizzle in the olive oil in a thin stream, whisking all the time. Stir in the shallot and the chopped herbs. The vinaigrette keeps for up to 2 days, tightly covered, in the refrigerator.

Basil Sauce

Yield: 2¼ cups

This fluorescent green sauce has all the qualities of a good sauce: great consistency, color, and flavor. Brigit Binns, my collaborator on this book, has been won over by its light, gentle flavor and tells me she now keeps small quantities of the sauce, made without the butter, in the freezer. When ready to use, she brings it to a simmer and whisks in the appropriate amount of butter.

▶ **1 cup dry white wine**
2 small cloves garlic, thinly sliced
1 cup Chicken Stock (page 186)
½ cup heavy cream
1½ cups loosely packed basil leaves
¼ cup milk
½ teaspoon salt
Freshly ground white pepper to taste
⅔ cup unsalted butter, cut into 10 pieces

In a medium nonreactive saucepan, combine the wine and garlic; bring to a simmer and reduce by half. Add the stock and return to a simmer. Reduce to two-thirds of the original volume, until 1⅓ cups of liquid remains. Add the cream and return to a simmer, then remove from the heat and set aside to cool, uncovered.

Bring a medium saucepan full of water to a boil. Add the basil and blanch for 2 minutes. Remove the leaves with a skimmer and, as soon as they are cool enough to handle, squeeze out as much water as possible. Immediately combine the blanched basil with the milk in a blender (this will stabilize the color of the basil). Blend for about 3 minutes, adding more milk if necessary to make the mixture move easily, scraping down the sides of the container as necessary. When the mixture is bright green and the basil is completely puréed, gradually add the cream mixture with the motor running. Add the salt and white pepper and strain the sauce into a clean pan. Cover and refrigerate until ready to use.

To complete the sauce, bring it to a simmer over medium-high heat. Stir in half the butter and continue to stir until all the pieces have been absorbed. Immediately remove from the heat and whisk in the remaining butter, whisking until all of the butter has melted and the sauce is emulsified. Taste, adjust the seasonings if necessary, and use immediately.

Red Wine Sauce

Yield: 2¹/₂ quarts

This recipe can be cut in half successfully, but I prefer to make all 2¹/₂ quarts and freeze the extra because it's so versatile.

▶ 1 tablespoon vegetable oil
¹/₂ pound beef shank, cut into ¹/₂-inch cubes
1 cup coarsely chopped shallots (about 4 large or 6 medium shallots)
1 head of garlic, unpeeled, halved lengthwise
12 cups dry red wine
12 cups Veal Stock (page 189)

Preheat the oven to 375°. In a large roasting pan, swirl the vegetable oil to coat the bottom of the pan and add the beef, shallots, and garlic. Toss together and then roast, stirring every 10 minutes for about 30 minutes, or until the mixture is browned and crusty. Transfer the beef and vegetables to a large stockpot and add 10 cups of the red wine.

Using the remaining 2 cups of wine, deglaze the roasting pan, stirring and scraping all the flavorful bits from the bottom and sides. Add the deglazing liquid to the stockpot and bring the mixture to a rapid simmer. Simmer until the liquid is reduced to one-fourth of its original volume, about 3 cups. Add the stock, return to a rapid simmer, and reduce by about one-fourth, until about 11 cups remain. Strain the stock through a colander lined with a double thickness of slightly dampened cheesecloth, pressing firmly on the solids to extract all the remaining liquid. Discard the solids. Store covered in the refrigerator for 3 days, or freeze for up to 6 months.

Balsamic Sauce

Yield: About 2 cups

As with all vinegar sauces, this is a very pungent accent for dishes that can stand up to lots of flavor. Used judiciously, as in my recipe for Asparagus Cornucopias with Lobster Medallions (page 57), it adds a lovely jolt of rich, biting flavor. But be forewarned: a little goes a long way!

▶ 1¹/₂ cups balsamic vinegar
3 shallots, finely chopped
1¹/₂ cups Beurre Blanc (page 38), warmed

In a small saucepan, combine the balsamic vinegar and shallots. Over medium-high heat, reduce to about one-third of the original volume, or until about ¹/₂ cup of slightly syrupy liquid remains. Stir this mixture into the warm Beurre Blanc and use within 15 minutes.

Basil Pesto

Yield: 1½ cups

Basil is a very delicate herb—it discolors easily. The discoloration is caused by oxygen and heat, so here are a few tricks to keep your pesto a bright, luminous green: Always try to process pesto as little as possible. If you use a food processor, chill the bowl and the blade in the refrigerator so they stay cool while you make the pesto. Make sure to cover the pesto tightly or store in an airtight container immediately after making it. The top layer will discolor faster than the middle and bottom layers. You can keep a thin layer of oil on top of the pesto to stop oxygen from getting to it and causing the discoloration, but every time you use some of the pesto you will automatically stir more of the oil into the paste.

2 small cloves garlic
1½ tablespoons lightly toasted pine nuts
2 cups loosely packed fresh basil leaves
¾ cup plus ½ teaspoon extra virgin olive oil
½ cup freshly grated Parmesan cheese
1 teaspoon salt
½ teaspoon freshly ground black pepper

Combine all the ingredients, except the ½ teaspoon olive oil, in a food processor and process until a purée forms, scraping down the sides of the bowl as necessary. Transfer to an airtight container and pour the remaining ½ teaspoon of olive oil over the pesto to cover. Cover and refrigerate until needed (the pesto keeps for several days, tightly covered, but loses its bright green color after the first day).

Cranberry-Apple Chutney

Yield: 6 cups

This chutney is great with turkey sandwiches, chicken, and venison. Be sure to serve it at room temperature so that the flavors are the most intense.

4 cups fresh or frozen cranberries
4 cups peeled, cored, and diced
  Granny Smith apples (about 6)
1½ cups sugar

Heat a large nonreactive saucepan over medium-low heat. Place the cranberries and apples in the pan and cook, stirring frequently to prevent them from scorching, until the cranberries burst, about 4 minutes. Add the sugar and stir until it has dissolved. Simmer until the apples are completely tender, about 5 to 7 minutes. Cool to room temperature, cover tightly, and refrigerate. The chutney keeps for up to 5 days.

Marinated Portobello Mushrooms

Yield: 2 to 2½ cups

These mushrooms are slightly vinegary, but I think that's one of their main attractions. The classic way to prepare the marinated mushrooms is to drain off the marinade and grill them until slightly charred. Then they can be added to a salad or sandwich, or served on top of a steak—there are so many uses for them. They're one of my favorite basics.

▶ 1½ cups balsamic vinegar
½ cup extra virgin olive oil
4 sprigs rosemary
3 cloves garlic, thinly sliced
1½ teaspoons freshly ground black pepper
½ teaspoon crushed red pepper flakes
1 teaspoon salt
3 very large portobello mushrooms
   (about 8 ounces each), stalks removed and
   caps brushed clean with a soft brush

In a medium roasting pan, combine the balsamic vinegar, olive oil, rosemary, garlic, pepper, pepper flakes, and salt and swirl to mix evenly. Add the mushroom caps and turn to coat both sides well. Place a glass pan slightly smaller than the roasting pan on top of the mushrooms and place several heavy cans or weights in it so that the mushrooms are compressed and completely submerged in the marinade mixture. (If there is not enough marinade to cover the mushrooms, add 1 more tablespoon of olive oil and 4 additional tablespoons balsamic vinegar, or more as needed, using the ratio of one part oil to three parts vinegar.) Let the mushrooms marinate in the refrigerator for 3 hours, then turn them over, replace the weights, and marinate for another 3 hours. The mushrooms keep in the refrigerator for up to 1 week.

Croutons

**Yield: 3 to 5 cups croutons,
depending on the size of the bread**

Some croutons are tossed with garlic, oil (or even butter), salt, and pepper, and sautéed or fried, but this is the simplest kind of crouton, designed to have flavor added afterwards. Use your favorite stale bread—or, more likely, whatever you happen to have on hand!

▶ 6½-inch-thick slices of stale bread (rye,
   multigrain, country loaf, or corn bread)

Preheat the oven to 300° and trim the crusts from the bread. Cut the bread into ½-inch cubes and spread evenly on a baking sheet. Bake until crisp and just golden, 10 to 12 minutes. Cool and store at room temperature in an airtight plastic bag.

Pickled Onions

Yield: about 2 cups

You should always have some pickled onions in the refrigerator!

▶ 1 pint pearl onions or 3 medium red onions
1/2 cup red wine vinegar
1/2 cup dry red wine (such as cabernet)
1/2 cup sugar
1 tablespoon mustard seeds
2 tablespoons black peppercorns
Pinch of crushed red pepper flakes
2 tablespoons kosher salt

If using pearl onions, bring a large saucepan of water to a boil. Add the onions and blanch for 1 minute. Drain in a colander. When the onions are cool enough to handle, slide off their skins. If using red onions, peel and slice them into 1/4-inch rings.

In a medium saucepan, combine the vinegar, wine, sugar, mustard seeds, peppercorns, pepper flakes, and salt. Stir over low heat until the sugar has dissolved. Add the onions and bring the liquid to a boil. Simmer for 5 minutes, then remove from the heat and let cool completely. Transfer to a sterilized glass jar. Cover tightly and use as directed, or store in the refrigerator for up to 2 weeks.

Tomato Sorbet

Yield: 2 1/2 cups

I first used this sorbet in a dish that features the things I like best about food. It was a crisp sweet-bread salad with baby lettuces, sour cream, and walnuts (see page 36). There are so many things happening in your mouth when you eat that dish— you have the sweet and sour, the hot and the cold, the crunchy and soft. This sorbet also appears in my shrimp cocktail (page 47) and is a great garnish for summer when you can get your hands on tasty, ripe tomatoes. Making it with bland, winter supermarket tomatoes would be a crime.

▶ 6 vine-ripened plum tomatoes, peeled and
  seeded (page 202)
1/3 cup Simple Sugar Syrup (page 192)
1 tablespoon freshly squeezed lemon juice
1 1/2 tablespoons tomato paste
1/2 teaspoon salt
1/4 teaspoon freshly ground white pepper
1 tablespoon finely chopped chives

In a blender or food processor, combine the tomatoes, simple syrup, lemon juice, tomato paste, salt, and white pepper. Process until completely smooth, scraping down the sides of the bowl as necessary. Transfer to a large stainless steel bowl, taste for seasoning, and stir in the chives. Place the bowl, uncovered, in the freezer. About every 15 minutes for 2 hours, remove the bowl from the freezer and whisk the sorbet. If ice crystals form, return the mixture to the blender or food processor and blend again. Cover and store in the freezer until ready to serve.

Curry Oil

Yield: 2¹/₂ cups

This pantry product appeals on three levels: it looks great on the plate, it adds a lot of flavor, and it's easy to make. If you want to make the color even more vibrant, you could add a tablespoon of turmeric.

¹/₄ **cup best-quality curry powder**
2 tablespoons water
1 tablespoon curry paste
2¹/₂ cups canola or grapeseed oil

In a large glass bowl, whisk together the curry powder, water, and curry paste into a thick paste. Whisk in the oil. Cover and let stand at room temperature for 12 hours, whisking thoroughly every hour for the first 3 hours. Pour through a fine sieve into a clean glass jar and cover tightly. Use as directed, or refrigerate for up to 2 months.

Basil Oil

Yield: 1¹/₂ cups

This pantry staple is a little more time consuming to make than the Curry Oil (see left), but once you see the color and flavor that result, you will be amazed. It will actually keep for a little longer than 2 days, but it does begin to lose its flavor. Make half or even one-quarter of this recipe if you will not be using very much.

6 to 8 cups loosely packed basil leaves
   (about 8 ounces)
1¹/₂ cups extra virgin olive oil

Bring a large saucepan of water to a simmer. Add the basil leaves and blanch for 2 minutes. Remove with a skimmer and drain on paper towels. When cool, squeeze out as much water as possible. In a blender, combine the basil with ¹/₂ cup of the olive oil and blend for 1 to 2 minutes, scraping down the sides as necessary, until very smooth. Add the remaining 1 cup oil, blend just until mixed, then pour into a large jar. Cover tightly and let sit overnight in the refrigerator. The next day, strain the oil through a double thickness of slightly dampened cheesecloth into a clean glass jar. Use as directed, or cover tightly and refrigerate for up to 2 days.

Spiced Oil

Yield: ½ cup

Ground coriander is easy to find; ground fennel is less common. If you can't find it, use a spice grinder or a coffee grinder to grind your own. (Make sure to thoroughly clean the grinder before using it for coffee again.) Grinding your own spices makes this oil much more flavorful.

½ cup extra virgin olive oil
1 teaspoon ground coriander
1 teaspoon ground fennel seeds
½ teaspoon ground cumin
½ teaspoon ground ginger
1 teaspoon hot paprika
Pinch of ground cloves

Combine all the ingredients in a jar, cover tightly, and shake well. Let stand for 24 hours at room temperature. Strain through a double thickness of slightly dampened cheesecloth into a clean glass jar. Cover and refrigerate for up to 2 months.

Nougat

Yield: 1½ pounds

Nougat is actually a candy, but it is widely used as a flavoring for baked goods and desserts. It is made in countless flavors and colors, and is often studded with nuts. This smooth variety keeps almost indefinitely.

2½ cups sugar
1½ cups light corn syrup
¼ teaspoon salt
¼ cup water
2 large egg whites
½ teaspoon almond extract
4 tablespoons unsalted butter

Generously butter an 8-inch square baking pan.

In a large, heavy saucepan over low heat, combine the sugar, corn syrup, salt, and water. Stir until the sugar has dissolved. Continue cooking, without stirring, until the syrup registers 250° on a candy thermometer.

Beat the egg whites to stiff peaks. With an electric mixer, gradually beat one-quarter of the syrup into the egg whites and continue beating until the mixture holds its shape. Continue cooking the remaining syrup until it registers 300° on the candy thermometer (the "hard-crack" stage.) Very gradually beat the second half of the syrup into the egg white mixture (this is easier if you have help) and again beat until it holds its shape. Add the almond extract and the butter and continue beating until the mixture is smooth, thick, and shiny.

Quickly spoon the mixture into the prepared pan, smoothing the top. Cool well, then invert the block of nougat onto a work surface. Cut the candy into 1-inch squares. Wrap each one in waxed paper and store in an airtight tin.

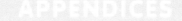

APPENDICES

Techniques

To clarify butter:

In a heavy saucepan, melt 1 cup unsalted butter (at room temperature) over low heat without stirring or disturbing the pan. Turn off the heat and, with a large flat spoon, gently skim off the white froth that rises to the top. Carefully pour the clear yellow "clarified" butter (about $3/4$ cup) into a container, leaving behind the milky white residue at the bottom of the pan. It's awkward to make clarified butter in smaller quantities than $3/4$ cup, but it keeps (covered) in the refrigerator for 2 or 3 weeks.

To deep-fry basil:

In a large, heavy saucepan or deep-fryer, heat 2 cups of vegetable oil to 300°. Plunge 6 to 10 completely dry sprigs of basil into the hot oil and fry, nudging occasionally to help them to brown evenly, for 2 to 3 minutes, or until crisp. Drain on paper towels and use within 1 hour. Cool the frying oil thoroughly, then strain and re-use.

To deep-fry carrot threads:

In a large, heavy saucepan or deep-fryer, heat 2 cups of vegetable oil to 300°. Peel 2 to 3 long carrots, then using the vegetable peeler, make long, thin strips of carrot. Cut the strips length-wise into $1/4$-inch-wide threads. Alternatively, julienne the carrots. Plunge the carrot threads or julienne into the hot oil and fry, nudging occasionally to help them brown evenly, for 2 to 3 minutes, or until golden and crisp. Drain on paper towels and use within 1 hour. Cool the frying oil thoroughly, then strain and re-use.

To deep-fry leeks:

In a large, heavy saucepan or deep-fryer, heat 2 cups of vegetable oil to 300°. Using only the white and light green parts of 1 leek, cut the leek in half lengthwise and rinse well. Pat dry and cut the halves lengthwise into long $1/4$-inch-wide strings. Again, pat the leeks completely dry with paper towels. Plunge the leek strings into the hot oil and fry, nudging occasionally to help them brown evenly, for 1 to 2 minutes, or until golden and crisp. Drain on paper towels and use within 1 hour. Cool the frying oil thoroughly, then strain and re-use.

To roast peppers:

Preheat the oven to 400°. Place the peppers on a lightly oiled baking sheet. Roast for 20 to 25 minutes, turning them over halfway through, until the peppers are softened and the skins are blistered and slightly blackened. Transfer to a large nonreactive bowl, cover the bowl tightly with plastic wrap, and let cool for 30 to 45 minutes. Peel the skins away and use as directed.

To peel and seed tomatoes:

Bring a large saucepan full of water to a boil. With a sharp paring knife, cut a small slit in the rounded end (not the stem end) of each tomato. Plunge the tomatoes into the boiling water and nudge them with a slotted spoon for 20 seconds. Remove and place in a colander under running water to stop the cooking process and prevent the flesh from becoming mushy. When cool enough to handle, peel the tomatoes, using the paring knife and starting at the cut in the end. Cut the tomatoes in half through the middle horizontally and squeeze each half to remove most of the seeds. Scoop out any remaining seeds with a small teaspoon, remove the core, and use as directed.

To cut herbs and greens into a chiffonade:
Stack about 5 leaves with their edges lined up.
Roll up the stack from one side (like a cigar)
and, with a sharp knife, cut crosswise into very
fine slices.

To make bell pepper juice:
Stem and seed 7 to 8 bell peppers, then process
pepper flesh in a juice extractor. Makes about
2³/₄ cups.

**To toast nuts (whole or sliced almonds, walnut
halves, and hazelnuts):**
Preheat the oven to 350° and spread the nuts
evenly on a baking sheet. Toast for 10 to 12 minutes, turning them over halfway through if they
are whole. The nuts should be just golden, as
this increases their flavor, but no darker or they
will be bitter. When toasting hazelnuts, remove
them from the oven and wrap in a kitchen towel.
Let rest for 10 minutes, then rub vigorously in
the towel to remove most of their skins.

To toast sesame seeds:
Place seeds in a heavy, dry skillet over medium
heat and toast, stirring frequently, for 2 to 3 minutes, or until golden. Watch them carefully so
they don't burn.

To blanch vegetables:
Blanching vegetables reduces their final cooking
times and, in some cases, allows a vegetable to
become brown and crisp that would have otherwise burned when grilled or roasted at high
heat. Depending on the final presentation of the
dish, vegetables are often transferred directly
from the blanching pan to a bowl of ice water
to quickly stop the cooking (called "shocking"),
thus keeping the vegetables crisp and retaining
their color. Blanching time varies for each vegetable, from 1 minute for fresh peas and snow
peas, to 4 minutes for new potatoes and french
beans, to 15 minutes for a medium turnip.

To cook beets:
Trim the tops and bottoms of the beets. In a
saucepan or stockpot, bring a generous amount
of water to a boil. Add the beets, cover, and
lower the heat to a simmer. Cook the beets for
25 to 40 minutes, or until tender. Remove with
a slotted spoon. When cool enough to handle,
slide the skins off.

Alternatively, roast the beets: scrub the surface
to remove any grit, then trim off the tops. Wrap
tightly in aluminum foil and roast at 400° for
1¹/₂ to 2 hours, or until tender. Cool and peel.

To section citrus:
Using a sharp knife, remove the skin and white
pith from the citrus. Hold the peeled fruit over
a bowl and, using a small, sharp knife, separate
the sections of flesh from the membranes,
catching the juices in the bowl. When you have
removed all the sections and set them aside,
squeeze the remaining membranes over the
bowl to extract any remaining juices.

Sources for Specialty Ingredients, Cooking Equipment, and Cookbooks

Mail-Order Sources

Chef's Catalog
3215 Commercial Ave.
Northbrook, IL 60062-1900
(800) 338-3232
Cooking equipment.

Dean & Deluca
560 Broadway
New York, NY 10012
(212) 431-1691
Specialty ingredients, cooking equipment, and books.

Kam Man Food Products
200 Canal St.
New York, NY 10013
(212) 571-0330
Asian ingredients and cooking equipment.

King Arthur Flour
P.O. Box 876
Norwich, VT 05055-0876
(800) 827-6836
High-quality flours and yeasts, plus baking equipment.

Sur La Table
84 Pine St.
Pike Place Farmers' Market
Seattle, WA 98101
(800) 243-0852
Specialty ingredients, cooking equipment, and cookbooks.

Weinessiggut Doktorenhof
Raiffeisenstrasse 5
67482 Venningen
Germany
(011 49) 6323-5505
(011 49) 6323-6937 (fax)
Fine-quality German wine vinegars.

Williams-Sonoma
P.O. Box 7456
San Francisco, CA 94120-7456
(800) 541-2233
(415) 421-5133 (fax)
Specialty ingredients, cooking equipment, and cookbooks.

Other Sources

Cook's Library
8373 W. Third St.
Los Angeles, CA 90048
(213) 655-3141
(213) 655-9530 (fax)
All new cookbooks, including special and foreign editions. Some recent out-of-print books.

Cost Plus
(510) 893-7300
Specialty ingredients, cooking equipment (including spätzle presses), and cookbooks. Call to locate a store in your area.

Cooking Classes

Cooking classes with Hans are occasionally held at Los Angeles–area cooking schools. Contact the restaurant at (310) 399-6504 for information about upcoming classes and other events.